The MYSTERY FANcier

Volume 2 Number 4
July 1978

TABLE OF CONTENTS

MYSTERIOUSLY SPEAKING 1
The Caper Novels of Tony Kenrick, by George Kelley. 3
Robert Rostand and Mike Locken, by Theodore P. Dukeshire. 4
Bowlers, Beer, Bravado, and Brains: Anthony Gilbert's Arthur Crook,
    by Jane S. Bakerman 5
Raymond Chandler on Film: Addendum, by Charles Shibuk 14
It's About Crime, by Marvin Lachman 15
Thomas Chastain and the New Police Procedural, By Larry L. French . . 17
The Nero Wolfe Saga, Part VIII, by Guy M. Townsend. 19
MYSTERY*FILE: Short Reviews by Steve Lewis. 30
VERDICTS (More Reviews) 37
THE DOCUMENTS IN THE CASE (Letters) 49

The MYSTERY FANcier
is edited and published bi-monthly by
Guy M. Townsend, 1120 Bluebird Lane,
Memphis, Tennessee 38116, USA. Contributions of all descriptions are
welcomed. Deadline for the September issue: 1 August 1978.

SUBSCRIPTION RATES: Domestic second class mail, $7.50 per year (6 issues); Overseas surface mail, $7.50; Overseas airmail, $12.00. Overseas subscribers please pay in international money order, check drawn on U.S. bank, or currency; no checks drawn on foreign banks, please. Make checks payable to Guy M. Townsend, not *The MYSTERY FANcier*.

Application to mail at second class postage rate
is pending at Memphis, Tennessee

Copyright 1978 by Guy M. Townsend
All rights reserved for contributors
ISSN:0146-3160

MYSTERIOUSLY SPEAKING...

You will have noted that even my urgent, pathetic plea in the last issue failed to shake loose a cover from the cold-hearted artists among us. Out of sheer desperation I am going to try to make a cover out of my certificate of membership in The Giant Rats of Sumatra, the only even vaguely mystery related item that I have been able to lay my frantic fingers on. I have no idea how it will work out, and I'm warning you folks--if you don't send me some cover art I'm going to dust off the infamous question mark and use it for a cover from here on out.

The delivery of TMF 2:3 appears to have been quite erratic, and therein lies a tale. To have mailed out 2:3 first class would have cost 54¢ per copy under the new postage rates. Even at book rate, which I probably couldn't have used, it would have been 36¢ each, a penny more than it cost to mail 2:2 first class. It was with these horrific figures in my head that I spoke to a friend of mine who edits a slick magazine here in Memphis (called *City of Memphis*, and surprisingly good), and he suggested that I look into the possibility of getting a second class mailing permit. That I did, and the upshot of it all is that TMF 2:3 was supposed to have gone out second class, while my application was pending. Now, postal regulations clearly state that a magazine need only be identified as going via second class mail within its first five pages. It does not have to be stamped "Second Class Mail" on the cover, nor are any stamps supposed to be attached--one just gives the mailing post office a check to cover the entire run. However, as a class, postal employees are probably the most incompetent workers on earth, and I have been getting copies of 2:3 back marked "returned for postage" since two days after I mailed the issue. If your copy of 2:3 has not yet arrived--and I fear that many of them may not have--let me know and I'll send another copy right away. I am very sorry for this poor service, especially since in the long run 2:3 is going to end up costing me more than it would have had I mailed it first class. Live and learn, I suppose, but if the permit ever does go through it should lower the mailing costs considerably.

One of the requirements for mailing at the second class rate is that the material be reproduced by offset or some better process. In other words, mimeo is out, which is why this issue is offset printed. No, I haven't acquired an offset press yet, but I'm going to as soon as possible, one reason being that this one issue alone is going to cost me nearly $150 to have printed, and I have to supply my own paper! With fewer than 150 paying subscribers you should have no truoble deducing that I am not getting rich putting out this publication. In fact, while I should recoup some of my expenses through future sales of back issues, I'm not even breaking even.

Therefore, effective with TMF 3:1, the subscription rate will be $9.00 for six issues, and, frankly, I don't care to hear any negative comments about the increase. If any of TMF's current subscribers feel that the increase is unjustified, kindly send me an SASE and I will send you explicit instructions as to what you can do with your cheap-skate opinions. At $9.00 per year I should eventually be able to pay for the required offset equipment and even at some distant point down the road, have a few dollars left over. You want to know what I intend to do with any future surplus? Stick it in my pocket, that's what.

The size of this issue is back to 60 pages, but the word count has jumped dramatically, owing to my reversion to reduced type. Since it is offset printed it should be much more readable than the reduced type of earlier, e-stenciled TMFs. Actually, the type is even smaller than in those earlier issues, being elite spacing rather than pica, but I hope there will be no objections. The word count of this issue appears to be about the maximum for future issues. I have been typing this issue, nights and weekends, for more than a month now, and putting out a larger issue would make editing and publishing TMF a full-time job rather than a (supposedly) part-time avocation.

Those of you who are tired of these frequent changes in TMF's format (I'm one of that group myself) can rest assured that no further changes are contemplated. The next step up is to have it typeset, and I'm damned if I'll get into that.

Speaking of changes, the observant among you will have noted that TMF and I have moved again, the fourth address for this magazine since its genesis less than two years ago. This will be the last move for a while, since we have bought this house (I've added a new hobby to my list--frantically trying to find enough money to make the outrageous monthly house notes) after several unsatisfactory years of renting. It will be nice to have a permanent address again at long last, and maybe the P.O. won't lose as many subscription checks now that it doesn't have to chase me all around town. But I despair of the P.O. ever doing better, even under the most favorable circumstances.

A disparaging word is in order. At the outset I declared that TMF would be open to all manner of opinions, and so far I have kept out of these pages only such things as were illiterate, irrelevant, or obscene. I have, in fact, been guilty of several editorial lapses, publishing items which would have been better left alone. Among these I must number several of Martin Wooster's reviews, including, regrettably, two of the three which appear in this issue. It may be argued that, having printed Martin's reviews, I ought not turn around and attack them, and I certainly agree that it would have been better for me to have refrained from publishing them, or at least to have edited them heavily; but I didn't, and I accept whatever blame and censure is owing to me for that omission. But I cannot refrain from commenting on Martin's truely infamous misconduct, however much responsibility I must personally bear for it. I will not rant on for pages, which I could easily do on this subject, but will confine myself to a few remarks and a restatement of what is acceptable in this publication.

For some reason unknown to me Martin has decided to make a minor career of abusing John Ball. As one who has respect and admiration for John's work, I have been uncomfortable with Martin's comments but hav used them anyway with the idea of allowing maximum authorial and critical freedom. But Martin's disagreeable attacks have gone too far. They have nothing to do with the quality of John Ball's work--they merely reflect Martin's personal disliking for john. Otto Penzler is another writer on whom Martin has chosen to pour his unreasoned scorn at every available opportunity, and in his review of *A Coffin for Dimitrios* in this issue he even makes an unnecessary and vicious attack on James Sandoe. Now, harsh criticisms have a place in our genre, as in any other, but two elementary rules must be observed--the book or author should deserve the abuse it is receiving, and the criticisms should be made in something which at least approaches being a gentlemanly or lady-like fashion, or, failing that, is at least civilized. Martin's assessment of his own god-like superiority has led him to excesses inexcusable in ordinary mortals. This is particularly annoying since Martin's own writing is wide open to criticism. For example, the affectation of British spellings is a common adolescent affliction, but most of its victims out grow it; Martin has not, and whenever I publish something Martin has written I must waste precious time changing his spellings back to the American versions most (continued on page 61)

THE CAPER NOVELS OF TONY KENRICK

By George Kelley

If Donald Westlake is the master of the comic caper novel, then Tony Kenrick ranks as an excellent sorcerer's apprentice. In six wild books, Kenrick displays a talent for the funny and the surreal.

Take his first book, *The Only Good Body's a Dead One* (Simon & Schuster, 1970); two nutty American comedians working the night club circuit in France stumble into a bizarre smuggling scheme when a man drops dead in front of the stage during one of their shows. The comedy is a little strained in parts but the chase scene made up of the comedians ripping off a coffin during a funeral with the angry relatives in hot pursuit is classic. I also like the infamous dancing bear.

Good Body has its flaws, chiefly lack of character development and forced humor at times. The overall result, however, is worth reading.

Caper is the name of the game in Kenrick's second book, *A Tough One to Lose* (Bobbs-Merrill, 1972; Bantam, 1973). It's the perfect rip-off: a gang of professional thieves skyjack a 747. With 360 passengers. And demand a mere 25 million dollars ransom; they also develop a foolproof method of collection of the $25 million.

But the kicker is: they make the plane and the people disappear. The solution is clever and you'll enjoy it. (The main problem with reviewing caper novels, or most mysteries in general, is I have to make most of the details sketchy in order to preserve your enjoyment of the plot, should you decide to read the book. Sorry, but that's just the way it is.)

Where Kenrick shows his flair for satire and plotting in *A Tough One to Lose*, he's hilariously funny in his next book: *Two for the Price of One* (Sphere, 1974, 1975).

The plot, again, is clever. A gang of professional thieves take control of a Navy destroyer in the waters off New York City. They point the five-inch guns at the Chase Manhattan Bank. A demand for $5 million is made at the bank. To stress their bargaining point, the gang orders an incendiary shell fired. It pumps into the bank and wipes out a floor.

The perfect bank job, right?

Well, as always, something goes wrong . . . .

In 1975, the master and the sorcerer's apprentice both brought out similar books about kidnapping; Donald Westlake wrote the humorous *Jimmy the Kid* starring the Dortmunder Gang. The beauty is the Gang uses a book by "Richard Stark" as a blueprint for their own caper. And Tony Kenrick brought out *Stealing Lillian* (McKay, 1975; Warner, 1976).

Stealing Lillian is a caper in reverse. The CIA knows that a band of terrorists plan to kidnap the child of a millionaire family. So they secretly replace the millionaire family with look-alikes who happen to be a small-time con man, and the con man's latest victim, and a nine-year old orphan who talks like a Marine drill sergeant with a bad hangover.

The plan works: Lillian gets kidnapped. But what happens next, nobody in the CIA expected . . . .

The Seven Day Soldiers (Regnery, 1976; Warner, 1977) starts out as a caper novel. Three small businessmen find they need more money. One of them comes up with a foolproof method of robbing a Swiss bank. By mail.

They carry out their plan and it works: they split a cool twenty thousand dollars. Then they get the idea of transferring *all* the funds in an account to themselves.

That works too. Only too well.

They find they transferred all the funds in a secret account of an exiled South American dictator: one hundred and sixty-seven million dollars.

And the dictator is a very vicious fellow. He wants his money back.

The three businessmen hid their families and then isolate themselves in a mountain retreat with a drill sergeant they hire to make them fighters in seven days. In seven days they just might have to fight the dictator and his twenty-four bodyguards, his private army.

Finally, we have *The Chicago Girl* (Putnam, 1976; Berkley, 1977). In 1964 a hooker with an English accent and lots of class became the lover of gangland leader Ziggy Kurtz. When Ziggy died, he left one request with his partner and best friend, George Devine: give his lover a stolen emerald necklace worth $800,000.

The problem Devine had was that the woman disappeared.

That takes us up to the present. Henry Redding, hotshot New York reporter, devises a scheme to con Devine into handing the emerald necklace over. Redding knows the insurance company will pay $400,000 to get it back.

The scheme is nifty, but as in all of Kenrick's books, things start to go wrong . . . .

Kenrick's books are good enjoyment. They're well written with tons of suspense. The early books, *A Tough One to Lose*, *Two for the Price of One*, and *Stealing Lillian* accent humor over plot; the later books, *Seven Day Soldiers* and *Chicago Girl*, stress plot over humor. Either way, I recommend all of them to you.

† † †

ROBERT ROSTAND AND MIKE LOCKEN
By Theodore P. Dukeshire

Born Robert Hopkins and educated in Los Angeles, Robert Rostand has both traveled widely and worked at a variety of jobs including working with an arm of the State Department in Washington, D.C., the Caribbean and Pacific Islands.

In Mike Locken, Rostand has created a series character who deserves more recognition than he's so far received.

Nothing is known about Locken's early life except he helped Castro oust Batista--then served two years in the Isle of Pines for "changing my mind."

Locken's first adventure, *The Killer Elite*, finds him working for SYOPS, the security section of the State Department guarding a Czech defector named Wrodny. Unknown to Locken, people in high places have plans for both. A free-lance killer named Hansen kills Wrodny and almost leaves Locken a eunuch. After he recuperates, Locken is assigned the job of getting an exiled African leader and his daughter out of England while three hired assassins try and kill them.

In *Viper's Game*, Locken finds himself on a Portugese island just in time for a native uprising led by a black militant named James Morais. Locken leads a small band of whites across the island to safety, and along the way he finds out who's really behind the uprising.

A Killing in Rome is Locken's latest adventure. This time he's hired by border-runner Max Gurtz who's been lured out of retirement for

(Continued on page 14.)

BOWLERS, BEER, BRAVADO, AND BRAINS:
Anthony Gilbert's Arthur Crook

By Jane S. Bakerman

> I prefer to stick to my profession of making crime pay--
> pay me, that is. Any time when you're in any difficulty,
> want someone to prove you were in Newcastle when you--and
> the police--know you were in the North End Road at the
> time of the latest smash-and-grab, just look me up at 123
> Bloomsbury Street. Crook's the name--Arthur Crook.[1]

So speaks one of the most fascinating fictitious detectives, the creation of Anthony Gilbert (Lucy Beatrice Malleson, 1899-1973).[2] Arthur Crook, defender of the meek and scourge of the British police, is great fun to hang around with, though, as a lawyer who specializes in getting clients free of murder charges, he would object to the terminology. Gilbert makes a deliberate effort to define Crook as an able eccentric, an anti-establishment type who functioned effectively long before the term became cant.

For roughly thirty years, Gilbert wrote about the adventures of Arthur Crook, and the novels are fun and exciting largely because of her characterization of their hero. Wisely, Gilbert saved just that role for Crook; he is never the protagonist of a story, but rather an unlikely rider-to-the-rescue. Because he appears primarily as part of a frame structure or as a healer of an unhealthy society, called in as one might summon a physician, Crook is never "used up", and though the plots tend toward the formulaic, the series is always interesting *because* Crook is not overused. This factor is a tribute to Gilbert's narrative skill, for Crook comes startlingly close to caricature at times, and yet is saved from it by touches of humor, tenderness--and cleverness.

The eccentric detective was created, apparently, as a deliberate contrast to the popular concept of the English-mystery-story detective.

> Anthony Gilbert says he invented Arthur Crook "as a
> corrective to the increasing number of highly-born
> (not to say titled) British amateur sleuths at that
> time swamping our fiction. Mr. Crook was short, stout,
> vulgar, wore brightly colored suits bought off the hook
> (where all the others went to Saville Row), drank beer
> as opposed to their highly priced and fancy-titled vin-
> tages, and drove a ₤10 car. He was forever free from
> the menace of a personal romance, which has spoiled so
> many amateur detectives, and he didn't live on ground
> rents and toy with death as a hobby. He, like his
> author, had a living to earn. In point of fact, I now
> have a very great affection for him, but then it is dif-
> ficult not to be fond of someone who has kept you in
> bed and board for upward of ten years."[3]

Because authors, like parents, aren't always completely clear-sighted about their own offspring, an examination of Crook's character and personality is in order. Since contemporary readers are not "kept in bed and board" by the character, his fictional personality *must* be in some way compelling; it is. It is steadily refreshing, steadily funny, steadily appealing.

The earliest novel under discussion here[4] introduces, however, an Arthur Crook less attractive than the image in the faithful Gilbert-reader's mind. As she learned her craft, Gilbert had the wit and skill to modify, to humanize, her earliest impusles. The original model smacks of arrogant boastfulness rather than disarming frankness: "'But give me the central court any day. I've got a lot of murderers off there. The atmosphere suits me,' he said in a blithe voice."[5] Not very likeable, a cold, tough cookie, the unmellowed Arthur is disdainful about the society in which he moves:

> It doesn't do in this country anyhow not to conform to type, and the Court will be full of people who are stuffed with detective stories and know that any one who doesn't have hysterics in the dock is guilty. All the old safeguards are down . . . . You daren't look a man in the eyes or have an alibi or be strong and silent—it's the day of the whimpering rat and the ferret. The dog, the trustworthy British, dependable dog, is simply nowhere. (*Experts*, p. 129)

This Crook is, apparently, reasonably well educated, as symbolized by the fact that he uses French easily and seemingly with a decent accent (*Experts*, p. 193). Even his physical description seems designed to be gross rather than bouncingly eccentric:

> One Arthur Crook, a slow-speaking, pot-bellied lawyer with a great circular face and a crafty eye. He had an eyrie of an office—he never spoke of it as chambers, though his address might be the Temple—and he wore snuff-colored clothes. He suffered from gout and had to walk with a stick. He had a tongue like vitriol and a voice like velvet. (*Experts*, p. 95)

Along with the stick and the gout, Crook's "roving eye . . . with a peculiar colorless intensity" was to disappear (*Experts*, pp. 95-96). And a good thing, too. It would have been a structural problem of almost insurmountable proportions to proceed with a major, continuing, essentially healing character whose personality and attitudes were so vigorously unappealing to the reader.

When Gilbert really hit her stride, then, the Arthur Crook who emerged and who appeared in a torrent of novels is cheeky, confident, the bane of the police, but the delight of his fans.

It should be noted, before we become submerged in the true personality of A. Crook, that among the many *outside* factors which humanize this amateur detective, two are of great importance. One is his aide, Bill Parsons of the mysterious past; a former wrong doer whom Crook has taken on as an assistant, Parsons is "a tall, unsmiling man with a ruined face and a slight limp where a police bullet had caught him in the heel several years before."[6] Always a figure of intriguing mystery, Parsons contrasts with and augments the bluff, open Crook characterization. The second of these crucial outside factors grows from Crook's habit of hanging about in pubs (where, as a matter of fact, he picks up a good many of his clients); Gilbert has a knack for adopting and adapting the most amusing of English pub names, and not the least among the books' attractions is the reader's interest in the beautifully rendered ambience of the succession of fascinatingly named pubs: The Bag O' Nails, The Two Chairmen, The Blue Bottle, for example.

But the major fascination lies, of course, in Crook himself, who becomes, in his perennially middle-aged prime, a vigorous fellow, bursting with energy, "what appeared to be the last of the rocket-bombs."[7] Along with that energy comes an ever undiminished attraction to and fascination with the human race; Crook thinks,

> No wonder you never got tired of life. He thought that
> if there was an eternity he could spend it in bliss
> just watching the world go by. There's nought so queer
> as folk and it was the queerness that held him in perpetual thrall.[8]

The lawyer never becomes a sex symbol, remaining, instead, simply cute in a rough sort of fashion. The roughness is stressed by the animal imagery Gilbert often uses. For instance, when he smiles, he's said to be giving "his imitation of a kindly alligator" (*Home*, p. 33), an image actually a bit overused. And one character, a young woman as earthy and as blunt as Crook himself, ventures this description:

> "Rum old bird,"' said Elsie. "Makes you believe in
> all that stuff about the missing link, though, doesn't
> he? I mean, put a gorilla in a hand-me-down suit and
> you put up the pair of 'em in an identity parade and
> no one could tell the difference."[9]

But gorilla-like or not, the ultimate Crook has abandoned drabness for vividness in his dress; though he continues to wear off-the-rack suits, they are always a bright brown, sometimes chestnut-colored, perhaps even glossy! (*Home*, p. 10). This sample description characterizes both his attire and much of his attitude:

> He pulled on his rough brown overcoat over his bright
> brown suit, jammed his brown derby hat over his red-
> brown eyebrows, turned up his coat collar, shoved the
> gloves he never wore into the pocket of his coat--a
> man in a fog is wise to keep his hands free--and
> walked out into the dark. (*Latch*, p.4)

In keeping with his taste in dress, vintage Crook is not an erudite Briton:

> "These educated chaps can't let well alone . . . . A
> lot of this education is hooey, and it's my belief
> it's all wrong stuffing it down people's throats. If
> chaps want to be educated they'll manage it somehow,
> and if they don't, then it's a waste of time and
> money." He didn't actually say, Look at me, I was
> never educated, a fact indeed which sprang to the
> least perceptive eye, but his manner said it for him.
> (*Bottle*, p. 109)

And his diction says it for him, too; for instance one of his favorite sayings is incorporated into his attitude toward the constabulary, "We ain't the police, praise the pigs"[10]--though we must remember that even the cagey Crook couldn't foreshadow the terminology of the Sixties! And the Crook most of us know has the kind of familiarity with French that evidently breeds contempt: "'Toosh,' said Crook, and Stuart stared. 'French,' Crook explained. 'BBC pronunciation.'" (*Bottle*, p. 136)

Crook is as unprepossessing--but clever--about his office and his apartment. The latter is a comfortable but not fancy flat at Number 2 Brandon Street.[11] We know more about 123 Bloomsbury Street where his chaotic office is located at the top of a battered building in that unsavory section; its location and its appointments reveal the pragmatic streak in Crook's personality:

> The front door of the building would remain open un-
> till he himself closed it on leaving. He had that

> arrangement with the landlords; a lot of his clients
> preferred paying their visits after dark and he and
> Bill took it in turn to stand in for each other to
> deal with the shady brotherhood who had christened
> Crook the Criminals' Hope and the Judges' Despair.
> . . . There was no carpet on these stairs and he
> could hear the feet . . . . If a chap thought it
> worth coming up eight flights on foot to consult him
> it showed he was in earnest. Besides, if you had an
> elevator the odds were that you'd have a night porter,
> too, and a lot of his clients liked to come at a time
> and to a place where the coast would be clear. (*Home*,
> p. 150)

The novels include a lot of talk about Crook's shady clientele, but they never feature a client guilty of the crome of which he (or more usually she) is accused. So much for Crook's purported flouting of the law! "You have the reputation of never losing a client—to the gallows, I mean. I have even heard you say that where the requisite evidence is not forthcoming you are prepared to manufacture it." (*Came*, p. 5) The manufacturing is much more talk than show, a part of Crook's shady character guise.

Another part of that guise is his sense of self-worth, now transformed into beaming, unabashed self-confidence; "Watch the papers," he says, "I shan't disappoint you. Where there's Crook, there's crime." (*Question*, p. 212). The self-confidence is kept from the original arrogance by the fact that it's laced with concern, "My motto is Crook always gets his man, and I only act for the innocent, so your troubles are mostly over" (*Bottle*, p. 81), and with joy in his work:

> "Matter of fact, this is just the sort of case I
> like. A nice cosy domestic murder. On the surface,
> everything looks so quiet and respectable, like that
> box belonging to who was it?—dame called . . . "
> "Pandora," suggested Stuart.
> "That's her. Well, you remember when someone
> lifted the lid out came all kinds of malice, hatred
> and all uncharitableness, everythin' in short, except
> hope.
> "And that," added he, modestly, "is me." (*Bottle*,
> pp. 77-78)

Crook is, in fact, hope, for each time far more respectable members of society unleash troubles such as blackmail and murder, hope, in the shape of Arthur G. Crook, comes along to set the topsy-turvey world to rights!

One of the qualities that makes Crook into a valid symbol for hope is that he is capable of righteous anger ("Crook, angry, could be as formidable as a dive bomber," *Came*, p. 196) in the face of pending injustice. And while his other personal qualities are also softening devices, they would not function if other characters' perceptions of him were not mostly positive. Gilbert takes care to incorporate these positive comments (even though some are humorous or ironic) so that the reader, identifying with the commentator, enlarges his soft spot for the attorney. His blatant antipathy for women and his supposed lack of charm are undercut just enough, for instance, when one character reports: "Sammy . . . says you're a charmer. He says you could have a harem if you chose, without any trouble." (*Latch*, p. 181) Also, it is through others, often, that Crook's reputation is presented or underscored:

> "Crook?" His face brightened. "Not Arthur G. of
> London, S.W. 5? Is that old walrus still on the war-
> path? That changes everything. Know who I'm sorry
> for now? Mr. Edward Poulden [a bad 'un]. He can be
> like those chaps in Revelation who cried on the rocks
> to fall down and cover them--it won't do him a mite of
> good. Crook 'ull come popping along at any minute
> with a charge of dynamite to blast the rocks, and per-
> sonally if it's a choice between Crook and a landslide,
> I'll choose the landslide. (*Question*, pp. 145-146)

And one character, nicely drawn and herself as sharp-tongued as Crook, identifies him as a kind of "rough-cut" citizen of the world:

> He pulled his hand out of his pocket and slammed some-
> thing down on the counter. It looked like an ultra-
> sized visiting card, and I suppose that's what you
> could call it, though I'd never seen anything quite
> like it, and I shouldn't imagine anyone else ever has
> ever. Except his other clients, of course. It gave
> his name Arthur G. Crook, and two addresses, one in
> Bloomsbury and one in Earls Court. Not that I'd have
> been surprised if they'd been the Antarctic Circle and
> the Equator. He was the sort of man who'd find him-
> self at home anywhere . . . . I picked up the card,
> fascinated. "Your trouble our opportunity," I read.
> And, "Working hours all around the clock . . ."[12]

These visiting cards, along with his appearance, his habits and his locale, outrage more sedate barristers. Yet, Crook's habit of scattering the cards among his acquaintances (met in pubs, on trains, on the street), proves profitable and endorses his theory that the average citizen never knows when he will need a lawyer. This display of bravado strikes confidence into the hearts of potential clients and disarms his opponents, who tend to think that no one quite so bluff and cheeky can be formidable. That is, of course, just what Crook intends, and the villains remain misled until Crook closes in for the kill!

Crook is brave without being loud about it, and even in moments of the most sexteme danger (when Gilbert's affection for her character shows most clearly) he remains practical and level-headed.

> He remembered there was a sharp bend at the foot of
> the hill, and at the rate she was going, even the
> Superb wouldn't be able to negotiate that. "Etern-
> ity, here I come," announced Mr. Crook, remembering
> with the clarity of desperation one of his Mum's
> favorite aphorisms about dealing with a fool ac-
> cording to his folly. Even at this extremity he
> couldn't really blame anyone but himself. A chap
> with the most rudimentary notions of preservation
> doesn't drive with his eyes shut, which was precisely
> what he had been doing.[13]

This moment of danger also reveals his love for his cars--his first, the Scourge, is an ancient, tiny, brilliant red auto, which looked "as though it had been made out of a couple of red biscuit tins." (*Home*, p. 10). When Crook sacrifices her to save the life of a client, his tenderness and his bravery are nicely rendered. Gilbert also, in this episode, invokes a kind of unlikely-knight-to-the-rescue portrait:

> He drove the gallant little Scourge into the sandy

waste. It was all he could do to coax her to stay
upright; she bucked, she bogged, she panted, but he
brought her from one hazard to the next as a skill-
ful and sympathetic rider persuades his horse to
achieve the impossible. (*Question*, p. 231)

It is impossible to think of Crook carless, however, and he immediately acquires another car, quite as distinctive, quite as flashy . . . and surprising roadworthy.

He drove himself in his latest acquisition, an ancient Rolls, high in the body, half the length of
the most streamlined monsters that were turning the
roads into horror, but guaranteed to pass most of
them at a pinch. Her color was bright yellow. . . .
"Me, I like a car you can't forget. Not so easy for
some absent-minded chap to drive off in it and swear
in court he thought it was his." He patted her hood
affectionately. "Can't be two like hre in the country," he said.
Of course, he adknowledged to himself, she wasn't
the Scourge, just as your new wife isn't the same as
the old, and the new dog can't compare with the one
you've lost. But a wife's a wife and a dog's a dog,
and this was certainly a car in a million. Probably
the car wasn't built that, in his estimation, would
be the equal to the Scourge, but this one would run
her pretty close.
"The Old Superb," he said affectionately, patting
her again. (*Question*, p. 245)

Because of Crook's fondness for his autos, Gilbert frequently and effectively employs a device that is mainly associated with films: the car chase. Gilbert handles the chases as nicely as Crook handles the machines--even when someone's cut the brake lines:

The Superb was winging her way downhill like a
drunken bird. The hill was long and pretty steep.
The Superb had been made in a day when everybody expected value for money, good solid metal and insides
made to last, not like the tin and wire contraptions
you saw all round you nowadays. Two-Ton Tessie ain't
in it with her, reflected Mr. Crook grimly. Mind
you, he hadn't the smallest doubt what had happened.
Cars like the Superb don't put themselves out of action for a pettish whim, they don't go on strike;
they're a lot more dependable than many of the human
agencies responsible for their make-up. (*Mask*, pp.
129-130)

The car chases lend excitement, a valuable addition, for the Gilbert novels are not bathed in gore, despite the fact that they are built around at least one and often several murders. Most of the blood is shed off-stage, and Gilbert relies on her characterizations and the car chases to bolster the pace and quicken the reader's interest.

Unlike such heroes as James Bond, Crook is vulnerable; he can make mistakes, and he can get hurt. This vulnerability is a further factor in the softening of his character. Once he reproaches himself bitterly for not outguessing the killer:

Crook said with sudden passion. "In a murder case
nobody's ever careful enough. I thought I was watch-

> ing every mouse-hole, but you see I was wrong. I
> thought I should be next on the list--seems tame not
> to try to do for the man who's out to hang you--I
> didn't think of being by-passed. I meant to pounce
> when that attempt was made, instead of which I've
> been caught napping. I can't do anything about it
> now, except just tie up the threads." (*Bottle*, 185)

The thrill of the car chases and his vulnerability come together at the end of the ruined brakes episode:

> The Superb didn't make the break-through he'd antici-
> pated, because the great bulk of the lorry was there
> to slow him down. It was a chance in a thousand, and
> like many reckless chances it brought home the bacon.
> And he needed bacon now as he'd seldom needed it be-
> fore. Automatically he'd shielded his head--hands
> were given man for more than lifting tankards--he'd
> shut off the engine without realizing what he'd done.
> He felt like a porpoise in a gulf stream, any moment
> he'd go over and over, always assuming porpoises
> haunted gulf streams. He heard glass shatter, and
> the world darkened, someone screamed, he couldn't
> think who. The lorry driver hadn't seemed the hyster-
> ical type, and anyway, hysterical night drivers don't
> last long on the roads of Britain. Crook wasn't, he
> assured himself, a murderous type, just a cozy, hard-
> working chap who liked his job, but at this instant
> if he'd had a carving knife in his hand, it would have
> been bad luck for the chap who'd put this insult on
> the Superb. (*Mask*, p. 131)

The very successful combination of chase and stream-of-consciousness is a sound example of Gilbert's skill in keeping her story moving and her character realistic.

Though Crook affects immunity from women's charmes, calling all of them "Sugar" in an attempt to categorize rather than individualize them, the bulk of his clients are damsels saved from distress--from execution, in fact. He disguises his fairly tender heart as he hids his cleverness, but a give-away avuncularity sometimes seeps through . . . invariably, he's responsive to women, perhaps especially those who are themselves vulnerable.

> "Take it easy," said Crook. He pushed forward a
> chair and persuaded her to occupy it. "The bad time's
> over. Just get that into your head." He put one
> huge freckled paw over those shaking hands. When he
> spoke like this you understood why he was so success-
> ful; his tone would have coaxed a hippopotamus out of
> its pool during a heat wave. (*Woodshed*, p. 236)

And in one of the latest of the novels, Crook really hits it off with an important witness; they respect one another and understand one another:

> May looked at him, wholly fascinated. It wasn't sim-
> ply gratitude that he'd got her out of a nasty situa-
> tion, it didn't even occur to her it might be a case
> of jumping out of the frying pan into the fire, she
> didn't think that angels come in strange disguises
> . . . she was simply fascinated, there was no other
> word for it. If he'd been Sir Lancelot and St. George
> for Merrie England rolled into one, she couldn't have

been more enchanted. And yet all she saw was a round
barrel of a man with popping bright eyes and red hair
and brows that wouldn't have shamed a fox. (*Mask*, p.
19)[14]

Having done a good job of humanizing the original Crook characterization, then, Gilbert has done a good job of preparing the reader to be intrigued with his philosophy and fascinated by his methods.

An important facet of Crook's philosophy is his firm conviction that England is the best place on earth.

"On the *Continong*," agreed Crook. He thought himself it was an odd predilection, but one shared by thousands of his fellow countrymen. For himself, he hadn't left his native land since returning to it with the utmost dispatch in 1918, after three years of dodging German bullets and shells, and he was inclined to remark that foreign parts were too damn dangerous for a chap who hoped to die in his own bed. (*Came*, 28)

He can wax poetic about his work, and often does:

Our case. Y'see it's like a cake. . . . Look how unromantic it is at the start, just so many heaps of flour and sugar and whatnots, whatever you put into cakes. But when it's been properly mixed and cooked, and the cookin's the important thing, especially about our cake, what a metamorphosis, as some chap has said. Light, tasty, highly flavoured, nicely-coloured, appetising, tempting, irresistible. Yum-yum . . . . Doesn't that start the digestive juices flowing? (*Bottle*, p. 95)

But he is never sentimental about a murderer, standing firmly for true justice, and being practical about the killer personality.

"It's vanity," said Crook. "Gets 'em all in the end. Remember that chap who kept drowning wives in baths? Got away with it once or twice and thought he could get away with it forever. . . . Everything would have worked out just fine if he hadn't got overconfident, and that's when chaps become careless.[15]

The Crook killer-catching method is blunt and to the point, and sometimes shaves off some of the niceties of life: "'You're offensive, sir.' . . . 'I'm being paid for it,' Crook explained, simply." It is "one of Crook's habits to take a bull by the horns. Why else . . . had the creatures been furnished with such appendages?" (*Bottle*, p. 83) Sometimes he verges on cruelty, but only when absolutely necessary: "It was brutal, but you can't afford kid gloves in his line. Knuckledusters, are more like it" (*Mask*, p. 122), and on at least one occasion he is abusive of hospitality in the interest of his client: "He foxed round the room, stopping to admire a recent photograph of his host which he presently slipped into his pocket. You never knew when a thing like that mightn't be useful. (*Home*, p. 75)

But Crook's methods always serve the right, as do his considerable might and his cleverness. And taken all in all, the characterization is much more human than devious, much more appealing than crass, and very great fun. In the long string of Arthur Crook novels, then, Anthony Gilbert has created a character whose charm, bounce, and skill grow nicely out of and away from his early manifestations. With the introduction of and emphasis upon the bowlers, the beer, the bravado and the brains, emerges one of England's most unlikely but most successful fictional detectives.

NOTES

[1] Anthony Gilbert, *Murder Comes Home* (New York: Walter J. Black for the Detective Book Club, 1951), p. 11. All further references are indicated in the text.

[2] Other Gilbert detectives are Scott Egerton and M. Dupuy. Malleson's other pseudonym is Anne Meredith.

[3] Anthony Gilbert, *The Innocent Bottle* (New York: A. S. Barnes and Co., 1949), inside back dust jacket leaf. All further references are indidcate in the text.

[4] The original English dates of publication and the original titles of works treated here are *Murder by Experts*, 1936; *Something Nasty in the Woodshed* (*Mystery in the Woodshed*), 1942; *Don't Open the Door* (*Death Lifts the Latch*), 1945; *Lift Up the Lid* (*The Innocent Bottle*), 1948; *Murder Comes Home*, 1950; *Is She Dead Too?* (*A Question of Murder*), 1955; *And Death Came Too*, 1956; *Death Takes a Wife* (*Death Casts a Long Shadow*), 1959; *Ring for a Noose*, 1963; *The Visitor*, 1967; *Death Wears a Mask* (*Mr. Crook Lifts the Mask*), 1970; *A Nice Little Killing*, 1973.

[5] Anthony Gilbert, *Murder by Experts* (New York: The Dial Press, Inc., 1937), p. 111. All further references are indicated in the text.

[6] Anthony Gilbert, *Mystery in the Woodshed* (New York: The Detective Book Club, 1942), p. 219. All further references are indicated in the text.

[7] Anthony Gilbert, *Death Lifts the Latch* (New York: Walter J. Black for the Detective Book Club, 1946), p. 107. All further references are indicated in the text. For the contemporary reader, a nice bonus here, as in many novels of the time, is the portrait of the wartime England of the indomitable spirit for which Crook is an effective symbol.

[8] Anthony Gilbert, *Death Casts a Long Shadow* (New York: Pyramid Publications, Inc., 1966), pp. 169-170. All further references are indicated in the text.

[9] Anthony Gilbert, *A Question of Murder* (New York: Random House, 1955), p. 134. All further references are indicated in the text.

[10] Anthony Gilbert, *And Death Came Too* (New York: Random House, 1956), p. 227. All further references are indicated in the text.

[11] Anthnoy Gilbert, *Ring for a Noose* (New York: Random House, 1964), p. 3. All further references are indicated in the text.

[12] Anthony Gilbert, *The Visitor* (Roslyn, NY: Walter J. Black, Inc. for the Detective Book Club, 1967), p. 19. All further references are indicated in the text.

[13] Anthony Gilbert, *Mr. Crook Lifts the Mask* (New York: Beagle Books, Inc., 1971), p. 130. All further references are indicated in the text.

[14] There is no hint of romance between Crook and May Forbes; they simply recognize one another as decent, responsible, caring human beings. A nice touch in the Gilbert novels is the procession of female characters like May who are capable, self-supporting, practical and forthright.

[15] Anthony Gilbert, *A Nice Little Killing* (New York: Random House, 1973), p. 246. All further references are indicated in the text.

RAYMOND CHANDLER ON FILM: ADDENDUM
By Charles Shibuk

Down These Mean Streets a Man Must Go (A Portrait of Raymond Chandler). Adapted and arranged from Raymond Chandler's writings by John Foster and Fred Burnley. Produced and directed by Fred Brunley for BBC TV. Narration: Glyn Worsnip. Research: Barbara Barkham. Assistants to Producer: Sarah Lidell, Eileen Brown. Designer: Richard Morris. Camera: Eugene Carr.
Cast: Tom Daly as Raymond Chandler; Edward Judd as Marlowe; Sue Lloyd as Linda Loring; David Bauer as Gregorious; Geoffrey Toone as Potter; Sarah Marshall as Muriel; Robert O'Neill as Ohls; Lillian Bronson as Cissy Chandler. (Credits supplied by William K. Everson.)

    Produced in the early 70's by the BBC, this TV film runs for about an hour. It has not, to the best of my knowledge, been shown in America, and is one more example of Chandler's high standing as a novelist, rather than just a mystery writer, in England.

    The usual biographical facts are noted, and Chandler's literary efforts are examined with penetrating insight into his creative process. Much of the narration from Chandler's inner monologues can be found in letters included in *Raymond Chandler Speaking*.

    There are also brief film excerpts from *Murder, My Sweet* and *The Big Sleep*, and a dramatization of a few scenes from *The Long Goodbye*--obviously made before the release of Robert Altman's 1973 film version.

    Of interest is some location shooting in La Jolla with Chandler ambling around and philosophizing, and the pathetic suicide attempt in the shower which is not quite as dynamic as Hitchcock's use of a similar location in *Psycho*.

    All-in-all an intelligent study of and a well-deserved tribute to one of America's most popular mystery writers.

† † †

(Continued from page 4.)
one last job.

    Vanya Kirovin, a deposed KGB chief, has written a diary and wants to defect. Burdened with a traitor, a mercenary who's lost his nerve, and a beautiful Hungarian agent, Locken crosses over the Hungarian border only to find an old enemy lying in wait.

    The main theme that runs through Rostands books is that the big of intelligence are just as vicious and treacherous as the killers Locken has to deal with.

    Rostand is also the author of *Vengeance Run* and *The D'Artagnan Signature*.

IT'S ABOUT CRIME

By Marvin Lachman

Before 1967 the publication of a book about the mystery story was a special occasion. Since the revolution launched by *The Armchair Detective* in that year, non-fiction works in the genre have become a minor growth industry. The latter part of 1977 and the early months of 1978 have been especially fruitful.

It may be inappropriate for me to review the first two books I shall consider since I was involved in the research necessary for their preparation. Still, the books are so outstanding that, with that caveat, I want to write about them.

In case you've been on Mars you may have missed Dilys Wynn's *Murder Ink* (Workman, $7.95), which achieved the unprecedented success of reaching Number 8 on the trade paperback bestseller list. *Murder Ink* can best be summed up in one word: "delightful", a word heretofore always used to describe Christianna Brand. It consists of more than 150 articles, some of which are attributable to famous names in the field. Others are either by Miss Wynn under her own name or under several obvious pseudonyms.

Make no mistake; this book is not perfect. It contains an occasional error. Ketchum's *Death in the Library* is not a Dell Crime Map, though it is Dell #1. The article called "Disposing of the Body" gives away too much of the plot of several books.

However, there is much more on the positive side. Clifford A. Ridley's article on reviewing is the best on the subject I've ever read. There's a fine article by Eleanor Sullivan on editing. There is a very clever interview with Donald Westlake under his four pseudonyms. Note especially his great line regarding Ross Macdonald.

The book contains an incredible amount of information, some of it totally useless. More is useful--e.g. diagrams of the hierarchy of the London and New York Police Departments and the location in London of the Edgar Wallace Pub. All of it is fun.

Purists might call Otto Penzler's *The Private Lives of Private Eyes, Spies, Crime Fighters, and Other Good Guys* (Grosset and Dunlap, hardcover, $14.95; paperback $7.95) "Son of *Detectionary*," but the book is so well done that it deserves to be considered on its own merits. Penzler has taken 25 of the leading characters in mystery fiction, written extensive biographies of them and then added complete checklists, filmographies, and scores of excellent photos and drawings. Most enjoyable and very readable.

The prolific Penzler also edited *The Great Detectives* (Little, Brown and Co., $9.95), in which the creators of 26 detectives give biographies of their creations, including fascinating descriptions of how they were conceived. Included are articles by Ngaio Marsh, Ross Macdonald, Ed McBain, Dell Shannon, Brett Halliday, and Nicolas Freeling among others. Bibliographies and filmographies are included.

Much of the popularity of detective fiction since the time of Holmes has been due to reader identification with series characters. Penzler's works should have a wide appeal.

There is much around in the way of author biography. Frank MacShane's 1976 *The Life of Raymond Chandler* is now available in Penguin paperback at $3.50. This is a good book, well-researched but marred by too much reliance on presumption where MacShane could not get the facts. Therefore, we get lines like "Chandler undoubtedly . . . ." and "Chandler must have . . . ." These flaws are more than offset by the

insights, based on extensive review of correspondence, we get into Chandler's personal life and his attitude toward writing. Incidentally, has anyone else noted the following similarities which I find between the lives of Chandler and Ross Macdonald:
1. Both lived in Southern California, though they spent considerable time in the U.S. Midwest and Canada.
2. Each had an absent father, and this lack was important to eache's personal life and viewpoint as a writer.
3. Each traveled extensively in Europe before becoming a writer.

Look for different similarities between Chandler and the subject of John McAleer's Edgar-winning 1977 biography, *Rex Stout* (Little, Brown, $15.00). Both were bookkeepers and successful businessmen until changes in their fortunes (and those of the nation's economy) forced them to take up writing as full-time occupations. McAleer has been criticized by Julian Symons for having adopted a factual approach with insufficient interpretation of Stout's character. But it is exactly that approach which makes this book so excellent. McAleer has done an incredible amount of research and presents all the facts in a well-organized manner so that the *reader* can decide what type of person Stout was.

Christie comes as the end. Added to a spate of prior books, there are three from Dodd Mead. In addition to Christie's own autobiography, there is the reissue of her 1946 *Come, Tell Me How You Live* and *Mallowan's Memoirs*, an autobiography by her husband. The latter two books deal with those times in her life when she went on archeological "digs."

A company which never published any of Christie's books nonetheless published an anthology of articles about her by some of the most prominent practitioners of crime writing in the United States and Great Britain. The book, *Agatha Christie, First Lady of Crime* (Holt, Rinehart and Winston, $12.95), was edited by H.R.F. Keating, who also contributed a portrait of Hercule Poirot. Christianna Brand, in her own inimitable style, provides a companion portrait of Miss Marple. Other excellent articles are by Philip Jenkinson on the films adapted from Christie works and J. C. Trewin on her plays. Julian Symons and Edmund Crispin, in separate pieces, dissect the deceptive simplicity of her work. The latter is especially good on why people read mysteries and their importance as a temporary escape from reality. (I know some people who probably rightly believe that mysteries are real, and the other aspects of life are the fantasy.)

Dorothy B. Hughes writes about the "straight" fiction Christie wrote under her Mary Westmacott pseudonym. Emma Lathen amusingly discourses on Christie's incredible American popularity. There are also articles by Elizabeth Walter, Michael Gilbert, Colin Watson, Celia Fremlin, and William Weaver. To these add a bibliography, some excellent photos, plus a marvelous caricature of our Aggie by Nicolas Bentley (artist, occasional mystery writer, and son of E. C. Bentley).

By this time you may have gotten the idea that this is a worthwhile book.

THOMAS CHASTAIN
AND THE NEW POLICE PROCEDURAL
By Larry L. French

A combination of the hard-boiled syndrome and the revised police procedural is found in the novels of Thomas Chastain. His recent credits include *Pandora's Box* (Mason & Lipscomb, 1974), *9-1-1* (Mason-Charter, 1976) and *Vital Statistics* (Times Books, 1977).

In *Statistics* Chastain purposely reveals the obvious, i.e. a concerted influence by Hammett and Chandler, during a sequence in which J. T. Spanner, the featured sleuth, and an "old-timer" private-eye discuss the case at hand. Upon learning that the latter worked for a number of years in California, Spanner inquires if the old man knew Philip Marlowe or Sam Spade and then comments: "They were both private investigators out there; Marlowe operated around L.A., and Spade worked in San Francisco. A couple of straight guys from all I've heard. They did a lot for the business."

Chastain, a former newspaper reporter and editor who lives in New York, readily admits that he was deliberately acknowledging the influence of Hammett and Chandler on his writings; but in fact he was trying to do more in terms of paying his literary debt to those two writers. Chastain intended that the book (which featured Spanner) should be a tribute to both writers. In doing this, he relied upon Robert Montgomery's version of the movie *The Lady in the Lake*, where the camera was used instead of the character of "Marlowe". This same technique is used in *Vital Statistics*, i.e., the use of the historic present, of removing all the "I saids", and the "I walked into the room." In other words, Chastain hoped to make the reader see the action at the moment it was happening to Spanner. The Hammett element was the existence of the "DeSancy Diamond", which was Chastain's version of the figurine, "The Maltese Falcon".

Two earlier books by Chastain, *Judgment Day* (1972) and *Death Stalk* (1971), have no relationship to his recent writings, which involve a New York City Deputy Inspector named Max Kauffman in the stories which concern the larger-scale "police procedural"; and Spanner, the private investagator, in the more intimate "private-eye" portrayals. Occasionally, Chastain mixes the two characters, but normally, one is the primary character with brief appearances by the other.

Chastain has also been influenced by Hemingway and the late James M. Cain, who has described Chastain's writing as "profound as well as exciting." And the late Grand Master of storytelling, John Dickson Carr, commented that Chastain's technique featured "expert storytelling as well as sound characterization."

Thomas Chastain was born in Sydney, Nova Scotia, Canada. He spend his early years in Florida, Georgia, Maryland and California. In 1958 he moved to New York City and decided that this most exciting and fascinating city would be his permanent home. Quite obviously, he has successfully utilized the "big apple" as the setting in his Kauffman/Spanner adventures.

Chastain has worked as a newspaper reporter and editor, and as a writer for magazines before turning to fiction full-time in 1973. A very active member of the Mystery Writers of America, Chastain edited the special issue of *Publisher's Weekly* for the 1978 International Crime Writers Congress in New York.

Chastain had planned for some time to do a private detective novel and had begun one before conceiving the plot for *Pandora's Box*.

Both private detective J. T. Spanner and Deputy Chief Inspector Max Kauffman are involved in this action-packed suspense thriller about a four-million dollar heist brought about in a most unusual way. The New York City Metropolitan Museum is the "scene of the crime", a man named "Conant" the ringleader, but two others (Griffith and Chilton) play key roles in regard to the solution of this particular mystery.

This book represents a combination "police-procedural" and "hard-boiled" detective story and clearly establishes Thomas Chastain as one of the best at what he does. *Pandora's Box* is further unique, in that it features a thriller with no villain . . . and a crime with no victim.

Chastain's preference for the "suspense" novel with New York City as the setting, again led to a new concept of the so-called "police procedural". His follow-up to *Box* is a super-thriller entitled *9-1-1*.

Again, the setting is New York City (during the Christmas season) with Deputy Chief Inspector Max Kauffman, N.Y.P.D. featured with Lieutenant John Tynan, who is promoted to Captain at the conclusion of this adventure.

The plot involves a "Christmas Bomber" and the frustrated efforts of the N.Y.P.D. to apprehend this insane destructor of New York's holiday season. J. T. Spanner, private detective, enjoys a brief but crucial appearance in this tight, expertly plotted and thoroughly well-researched novel.

Beginning with Macy's Thanksgiving Parage, the "bomber" commences his own version of the "Twelve Days of Christmas", notifying the public officials of the impending doom by utilization of the emergency telephone number, "9-1-1". The hopeless frustration of a city faced with a madman is ever-present in this "police procedural" and Chastain provides a close insight to the personal lives of those who live the day-to-day burden of keeping the country's largest and most exciting city safe.

At the conclusion, there is incorporated a sudden "twist of events", which leaves the reader totally breathless, after an outstanding build-up of realism, terror and tension. Kauffman, who is independently wealthy and maintains a mistress, along with a very dependent family, finds himself tempted to "use" his position as a police officer to his own advantage. Although subjected to political pressure and public outcry, he manages to keep himself within perspective and a sudden chain of events causes Kauffman to perform heroics somewhat "beyond the call".

An early conception of a "Spanner" story was set aside for the future, but perhaps in its place came *Vital Statistics*, in which the author shares with his readers data and anecdotes about New York City, while spinning an exciting yarn.

Featured again is the hero of *Box*, private detective (and former cop) J. T. Spanner, who is believable except for the fact that he employs his two ex-wives and apparently offsets his alimony payments accordingly. Otherwise, Spanner is competent, cool, and cooperative with his former colleagues, New York's finest.

Statistics deals with the disappearance of a young airline stewardess and her "alleged" boy friend. Spanner, during his search, encounters a drug operation, smuggling ring, stolen corpse and a corker of a surprise ending. The characterization is excellent and the story moves along at a swift pace and culminates quickly, but logically. Thomas Chastain is one of the best of the "hard-boiled" writers working in the profession today, and the lover of mystery and suspense fiction can find comfort in Chastain's preference to "take quite seriously" his role as an author within the genre.

THE NERO WOLFE SAGA
Part VIII

By Guy M. Townsend

[An Apology: Thus far in preparing the chapters of the Saga I have depended heavily on Baring-Gould's chronology and dating. As in most other facets of his book, Baring-Gould is grossly inaccurate on these matters, as I began to discover as I progressed further along in the series. Some of his inaccuracies I have caught; others--too many others--have slipped past me, as I discovered in reading John McAleer's biography. Unfortunately, I lack the time even to go back and correct those chapters which I have already written up but which have not yet appeared in TMF--I'm through *Champagne for One* (1958), now, though it will be some time before it makes it into these pages--so the Baring-Gould induced errors will persist until that point. I will, of course, make the corrections in whatever future form the Saga may appear, but all I have time for now is this apology.]

The Black Mountain [Baring-Gould dates this 11-19 March 1954, which is ridiculous; the episode lasts at least a month], published in 1954.
THE STORY ::: Marko Vukcic, Nero Wolfe's oldest friend, is shot to death outside the building in which he was living (the third floor of Rusterman's "had been remodled a year or so previously to provide an office in front and three private dining rooms to the rear"). Wolfe natura-ly determines to catch his murderer, but things do not go smoothly. It appears that Marko was heavily involved with a group aiming at the liberation of Montenegro, and Wolfe's "daughter", Carla (who is involved with the same group), contends that he was knocked off on orders from Moscow or Belgrade. Several weeks pass and still no progress is made, and when Wolfe receives a cryptic message saying the murderer is in Montenegro he unhesitatingly resolves to pursue him there, travelling by plane to Italy and entering Yugoslavia illegally via boat across the Adriatic. Wolfe and Archi's adventures in Montenegro are too far fetched for easy or comfortable belief. If I regarded the Saga as fiction, rather than the lives and exploits of real people headquartered in the old brownstone on West 35th St., I would say that the Montenegrin adventure combines all the worst elements of Manning Coles and Edgar Rice Burroughs. As it is, I will pass over this part of the story with an embarrassed silence, remarking only that Wolfe gets his man and brings him back to New York to stand trial. Though, as the balance of this discussion will show, *The Black Mountain* is overflowing with Saga developments, the story itself is not particularly satisfying, perhaps because Wolfe's activities in it are so grossly atypical.
WOLFE ::: First, the question of Wolfe's birthplace is finally and firmly established. Whatever his reasons for pretending to be a native-born American in *Over My Dead Body*, he was in fact born in a two story stone house on the side of the Black Mountain from which Montenegro takes its name. He states this explicitly and even points out the house (now empty and deserted) to Archie. His "daughter" says, "It is true you have Montenegrin blood," and to secure his passport he presents a certificate of naturalization, not a birth certificate. That latter point clinches it, really, because there is no reasonable way in which a native-born American can acquire (or need) a certificate of

naturalization. Even if he were born of American parents living abroad, his birth certificate and documentary proof of his parents' nationality are all that would be necessary to establish his citizenship. Apparently Wolfe remained in Montenegro until he was a young man. Archie says he played there with Marko when they were young boys, and Wolfe himself says "I was nine years old the first time I climbed the Black Mountain." Wolfe's active involvement there in matters political appears not to have ceased with the end of WWI as we have previously been led to believe. His contact in Italy during *The Black Mountain* episode is one Paolo Telesio--"In nineteen twenty-one he killed two Fascisti who had me cornered." When Archie says, "I thought you were Montenegrin. What were you doing in Italy?" Wolfe replies, "In those days I was mobile. . . . I'm not going to give you an account of my youthful gestes." A measure of the degree of his mobility can be found in his statement that "I have crossed this sea [the Adriatic] eighty times."

Marko Vukcic is Wolfe's "oldest friend" and, though Wolfe presents a bold front, he is obviously deeply effected by his death. When Archie tells him Marko is dead, "a corner of his mouth twitched, and after a moment twitched again." He sends Archie to the morgue to make the identification, but he soon follows: "That was the one and only time Nero Wolfe had ever seen the inside of the morgue." There, he places two old dinars over Marko's eyes--"To fulfill a pledge made many years ago"--and then says, "That's all. I have no further commitment to the clay. Come Archie." Wolfe had come to the morgue in a taxi, and he and Archie use the same machine to travel from the morgue to the scene of the crime; "That taxi ride uptown broke a precedent. Wolfe's distrust of machinery is such that he is never in a condition to talk when he is being conveyed in something on wheels, even when I am driving, but that time he mastered it. He asked me questions about Marko Vukcic." Archie is exaggerating here--Wolfe usually *does* talk while in moving wheeled vehicles, frequently to express his abhorence of said transportation. Archie is also mistaken in the following: "Since that was the first time to my knowledge that he had ever started investigating a murder by a personal visit to the scene of the crime--not counting the occasions when he had been jerked loose by some other impulse, such as saving my life--I was curious to see how he would proceed. It was a chance he had seldom had." In fact, Wolfe makes personal visits to the scene of the crime in *Some Buried Caesar, Too Many Cooks*, and "Black Orchids", to mention only three cases which spring immediately to mind. Nevertheless, this action *is* unusual, and it is rendered doubly so when Wolfe resolves to walk from the scene to Rusterman's: "The death of his oldest and closest friend had certainly hit him hard. He would have to cross five street intersections, with wheeled monsters waiting for him at every corner, ready to spring, but he strode on regardless, as if it were a perfectly natural and normal procedure." This is only the beginning, as Wolfe does, for him, an extraordinary amount of travelling in this episode, and not just by car. In order to expedite the issuance of his and Archie's passports he actually *flys* to Washington and back again, and of course he flys to London and then to Rome via commercial planes, and then from Rome to Bari, Italy, via light aircraft. However, these outstanding feats of courage do not indicate that he has cast off his phobia: "Wolfe was not taking it like a man. I had expected him to quit being eccentric about vehicles, since he had decided to cross an ocean and a good part of a continent, and relax, but there was no visible change in his reactions. In the taxis he sat on the front half of the seat and gripped the strap, and in the planes he kept his muscles tight. Apparently it was soo deep in him that the only hope would be for him to get analyzed, and there wasn't time for that. Analyzing him would take more like twenty years than twenty hours." Archie later relents somewhat, saying, of Wolfe's misery during the Atlantic crossing, "I admit he didn't make a show of it." Once Wolfe arrives in the familiar territory of his youth he undergoes a moderate transformation, becoming much more a man of action. In the night crossing of the Adriatic by small boat Wolfe is relaxed and comfortable, and in the five or so hours from midnight onward when they trek about the Montenegrin countryside he displays a remarkable memory of the geography and topography of Montenegro, and an unexpected degree of stamina. True, he suffers for it, particularly in his feet, but what he accomplishes is impressive indeed. In fact, Wolfe even does a considerable amount of mountain climbing in this one and bears up under it quite well. Wolfe is prepared for violence as well as physical exertion, carrying with him two knives: "He put one in a sheath on his belt, and strapped a shorter one to his left leg just below his knee. That gave me a better idea of the kind of party we were going to, since in all the years I had known him he had never borne any weapon but a little gold penknife." (Archie is forgetting Wolfe's Pete Roeder incarnation.) The knives are not just for show, either; when he and Archie find themselves in a tight spot Wolfe goes into action--"Wolfe, with his knife still at belt level, was advancing on him step by step, leaning forward in a crouch." Obviously, he knows what he's doing. Though Wolfe is in his own element here, and though Archie is handicapped by his ignorance of any language but English to the point of having to leave everything to Wolfe ("The basic setup between him and me was upset, and I didn't like it."), Wolfe still needs Archie: "If I hadn't let you grow into a habit I could have done this without you"; "There are good reasons why it would be better for you to stay here [in Italy], but confound it, you've been too close to me too long. I'm too dependent on you. However, the decision is yours." Of course Archie goes, posing as Wolfe's son. Both men, incidentally, take cyanide capsules along for quick suicides should the need arise.

The nature of the case gives Wolfe numerous opportunities to expound on politics and such:

> I condemn clichés, especially those that have been corrupted by fascists and communists. Such phrases as "great and noble cause" and "fruits of their labor" have been given an ineradicable stink by Hitler and Stalin and all their vermin brood. Besides, in this century of the overwhelming triumph of science, the appeal of the cause of human freedom is no longer that it is great and noble; it is more or less than that; it is essential. It is no greater or nobler than the cause of edible food or the cause of effective shelter. Man must have freedom or he will cease to exist as man. The despot, whether fascist or communist, is no longer restricted to such puny tools as the heel or the sword or even the machine gun; science has provided weapons that can give him the planet; and only men who are willing to die for freedom have any chance of living for it. . . . I make my contributions to the cause of freedom--they are mostly financial--through those channels and agencies that seem to me most efficient.

Wolfe is vigorous in his condemnation of communist tyranny in Montenegro, and at one point he says, "These vulgar barbarians have no right to degrade a history and deform a culture." At another he speaks of "the intolerable doctrine that man's sole responsibility is to his ego.

That was the doctrine of Hitler, as it is now of Malenkov and Tito and Franco and Senator McCarthy; masquerading as a basis of freedom, it is the oldest and toughest of the enemies of freedom. I reject it and condemn it." Wolfe has another encounter, not pleasant, with the FBI, this time in the person of a high ranking agent named Stahl who comes around to demand that Wolfe tell all he knows about the matter. When he arrived "Wolfe even did him the honor of rising to shake, which showed how desperate the situation was." Wolfe tells him, "I've been hunting the murderer of Marko Vukcic for eight days now [this is well before the departure for Montenegro], and am floundering in a bog, and if there is any chance you can offer a straw I want it." So he gives Stahl what he wants and then says, "Now I would appreciate a straw. With your prerogatives and resources, you must have one to toss me." This was hard for Archie to take--"I have never heard or seen him being abject before, and in spite of the strain he was under I didn't care for it." Stahl, who Wolfe had even allowed to search the South Room to assure himself that no one was hiding there, doesn't deign to reciprocate Wolfe's spirit of co-operation and leaves without giving Wolfe anything. But Wolfe's bad relations with the FBI do not extend to all branches of the government: "There were at least two VIPs in Washington, one of them in the State Department, whose ears were accessible to Wolfe on request," and the State Department VIP is called on to expedite the issuance of passports when the need for them arises.

Wolfe's dislikes get a pretty active workout in this episode. "Wolfe refuses to sit at table [sic] with one who has to pack it in and run." Wolfe: "Business shall not intrude on meals." "It irritated Wolfe to see good food turned down." He is "allergic to handshaking." Wolfe: "I look at people when I talk to them, and I don't like to stretch my neck." And he is not fond of children: "The day Wolfe would like to climb steps to look at children will be the day I would like to climb Mount Everest barefooted to make a snowman." Wolfe had been in the habit of dining at Rusterman's once a month (and Marko dined at the brownstone once a month also). In Marko's will Wolfe is named "executor of his estate and trustee ad interim," responsibility which he takes quite seriously: "We had dined nine times at Rusterman's [in the days immediately following Marko's murder], and Wolfe had insisted on paying the check, which probably broke another precedent--for an executor of an estate. Wolfe went early to spend an hour in the kitchen, and twice he raised hell. . . . I would have suspected he was merely being peevish if the look on the chefs' faces hadn't indicated that he was absolutely right." On another matter relating to food, Wolfe breaks his rule about eating before bedtime--at two o'clock in the morning after Marko's death he declares, "I'm hungry. I was in the middle of dinner when the news came of Marko's death. It took my appetite. I tried to finish anyway, but I couldn't swallow. With an empty stomach, I'm a dunce, and I'm going to the kitchen and eat something." That something is turkey, cheeze and pineapple. Later that same morning he declares, "I'm thirsty. Archie? Beer, please. Two bottles." He does not use the buzzer (presumably because Fritz has gone to bed [though we have previously been told that Fritz never goes to bed before Wolfe does]), and this is the first recorded time he has sent Archie after his beer. Wolfe is so annoyed in this case by the lack of progress that he displays his temper in an unusually violent fashion: "He shoved the paperweight off with such enthusiasm that it rolled across the desk and off to the floor. Then he picked up the pile of mail, squeezed it into a ball between his hands, and dropped it into his wastebasket. Of course it was childish, since he knew darned well I would retrieve it later, but it was a nice gesture, and I fully appreciated it." Wolfe is, in fact, so desperate for a lead that he goes "downtown twice to conferences at the DA's office." Archie says that Wolfe "had been making a living as a private detective in Manhattan for more than twenty years," but we already knew this because his first recorded case took place in 1933. Archie says he knew of only ten men "that Nero Wolfe called by their first names." Wolfe says "pfui" [Archie says "phooey"], and he also remarks that "Gallantry is not always a lackey for lust," and he speaks of "the miasma of distrust." Wolfe's yellow pjs, yellow sheets and black silk coverlet reappear and are joined by a newcomer to Wolfe's bedroom--an electric blanket. Wolfe is reading *But We Were Born Free* by Elmer Davis in this one, his weight is still one-seventh of a ton, and we learn that he speaks eight languages. English is one, of course, and Italian, Serbo Croat and Albanian are named. The other four are not too hard to guess: German, because of his dealings with the Austrian government; Turkish and Greek because of th eir close association with Montenegro; and French, because Wolfe is a civilized man. Wolfe (and Archie) gets thrown into an Italian jail for lack of papers, and Wolfe ends up getting shot in the leg before this episode is over because he wants to grandstand it.

ARCHIE ::: While they are out of the country Archie is obviously at a disadvantage, and he doesn't like it. His provincialism reemerges; he makes fun of the way the English speak English, and he refers to the speech of non-English speakers as "jabbering". He does, however, make himself useful to Wolfe, at one point earning a "very satisfactory" from him, and at another shooting it out with a bunch of baddies, killing all three of them. Although Wolfe withholds nothing from him in this episode, Archie remarks: "I'd like to have a nickle, or make it a dime, with the dollar where it is--for every item Wolfe has withheld from me just for the hell of it." After escorting FBI agent Stahl to the door, Archie remarks to Wolfe: "There are times when I wish I hadn't been taught manners. It would have been a pleasure to kick his ass down the stoop." This is the roughest language Archie has ever used in Wolfe's presence. Archie again mentions having "made a rule years ago never to leave on an errand connected with a murder case without a gun." In this case it's the Marley .32. Wolfe asks Archie, "Who is more trustworthy, Saul or you?" and Archie replies, "I would say Saul. I have to watch myself pretty close." As this episode opens Archie is preparing to leave for a basketball game at the Garden, so we may add that sport to his list of athletic interests. Archie mentions, as I believe he has done once before, that he doesn't care for the smell of the morgue. He says he spends "an hour or so each month looking at the pictures in the *National Geographic*." And finally, he uses the word "amanuensis."

OTHER REGULARS ::: "Fred Durkin knows how to dig, Orrie Cather is no slouch, Saul Panzer is the best operative north of the equator." Fred and Orrie don't play very large roles in this one, though we do see Fred sitting in the red leather chair again. Saul's role is not much bigger; he does remain in Wolfe's office, while Wolfe and Archie are out of the country, to answer the phone and such. Lily Rowan and Nathaniel Parker are just mentioned. Purley Stebbins is around, as is Cramer: "His big round face was a little redder, and his cold gray eyes a little colder, when he was exercising restraint." Bad old Rowcliff gets mentioned, too: "Among all the array of Homicide personnel that Wolfe and I have had dealings with, high and low, Lieutenant Rowcliff is the only one of whom I am dead sure that our feelings are absolutely reciprocal. He would like to see me exactly where I would like to see him." Marko, of course, is a central character, though he is dead throughout this one. Of him Wolfe says, "Mr. Vukcic had no close relatives, and none at all in this country," which delivers a pretty sound blow to the head of Baring-Gould's contention that Wolfe and Marko were brothers. The only one of Marko's relatives that we meet is his nephew, Danilo Vukcic, in Montenegro. In his will Marko leaves Rusterman's, his "only substantial asset", to six of his employees, the largest shares going to "Felix, Leo, and Joe." We learn nothing of Leo and Joe, but we are told a bit about "Felix Martin, a wiry, compact little guy with quick black eyes and gray hair." He is married and has four children, and of his voice Archie says, "You didn't expect a voice so deep from one that size, even after you were acquainted with it." We also learn more about Wolfe's "daughter", Carla. After first appearing in *Over My Dead Body*, "she had announced that she didn't intend to return to her native land, but neither did she intend to take any advantage of the fact that she had in her possession a paper, dated Zagreb years before, establishing her as the adopted daughter of Nero Wolfe. She had made good on both intentions, having got a job with a Fifth Avenue travel agency, and having, within a year, married its owner, one William R. Britton. No friction had developed between Mr. and Mrs. Britton and Mr. Wolfe, because for friction you must have contact, and there had been none. Twice a year, on her birthday and on New Year's Day, Wolfe sent her a bushel of Orchids from his choicest plants, but that was all, except that he had gone to the funeral when Britton died of a heart attack in 1950." The fact is, "Carla found Wolfe as irritating as he found her." One is inclined to sympathize more with Wolfe than with his "daughter". At least he treated her with what was for him extraordinary courtesy--"Wolfe went and took her hand and bowed over it"--while she behaved like such a perfect ass throughout that one is not exactly grief-stricken to learn of her death at the hands of the bad guys. Wolfe's contact in Paris is named Bodin; we only hear of him in this case, and I do not believe he ever appears again. We have, however, encountered his London contact before, in *Over My Dead Body*, where he was named Englebert Hitchcock. This time he is called Geoffrey Hitchcock, and he meets Wolfe and Archie at the airport in England on their way to Italy. "We hadn't seen him since he had last been in New York, three years before, and he greeted us cordially for an Englishman." Lastly, Fritz is present as always, and this time he earns a high compliment from Wolfe. After Wolfe learns of Marko's death Fritz remarks, "Starving the live will not profit the dead." Wolfe says, "I've never heard that before. Montaigne?" and when Fritz replies that he made it up himself Wolfe says, "I congratulate you. . . . To be taken for Montaigne is a peak few men can reach."

PHYSICAL ASPECTS ::: In the office Wolfe's chair is mentioned-- "the only one in the world he thoroughly approved of"--as is the TV and the "thirty-six-inch globe." Archie says there are two paperweights on Wolfe's desk, but he only describes one of them: "A hunk of carved ebony that had once been used by a man named Mortimer to crack his wife's skull." Upstairs on the third floor we are told that the South Room is "nice and sunny" and that it has a closet and its own bath. We also learn that it is "just down the hall" from Archie's room, which means that the rooms do not face each other across a central hall. Regarding the sceond floor there is another mention of "the gong that splits the air if anyone steps within ten feet of the door of Wolfe's room at night," and we learn the location of the telephone in Wolfe's bedroom: "He refuses to concede the possibility that he will ever be willing to talk to the phone while in bed, so the only instrument in his toom is on a table over by a window." Finally, "the sedan" is mentioned, but no make or model is given.

ROUTINE AT THE BROWNSTONE ::: Archie opens "the door with my key. After Wolfe had crossed the threshold I closed the door and put the chain bolt on." Note that, despite Wolfe's previously mentioned directions, the chain bolt was *not* on when they arrived. One other itme: "Ordinarily when I am out of the house and phone in Fritz will answer after two or three signals or Wolfe will answer after five or six."

ODDS AND ENDS ::: The bank balance is "a little over twenty-six thousand."

"When a Man Murders . . . " [May 1954], published in *Three Witnesses*, 1956.

THE STORY ::: Caroline Karnov waited two years after her husband Sidney was reported killed in Korea before marrying Paul Abury. Under Karnov's will she inherited nearly a million dollars, much of which she and her second husband tied up in a new car agency. When Karnov turns up in New York alive, Paul Aubry and Caroline, who is not his legal wife, hire Wolfe to make Karnov the following offer: they will return to him every penny they have left of Caroline's legacy, and will turn over to him complete ownership of the agency, if he will divorce Caroline so that she and Paul can be legally married. Archie goes to Karnov's hotel room to make the offer but finds him dead, and Wolfe has to find the murderer among the several people who benefitted from Karnov's first "death" enough to arrange his second. The deduction by which Wolfe settles on the guilty party is neat though not too well hidden, but the conclusion is not very satisfying or convincing, as Wolfe offers no proof that the murderer actually did it.

WOLFE ::: "Wolfe's reaction to an emotional appeal from a man is rarely favorable, and from a women, never." Wolfe expresses his distaste for talking with people who are standing while he is sitting-- "my neck is not elastic." Wolfe says, "I have on occasion welcomed an opportunity to plague the police, but never merely for pastime." When a woman who nearly breaks down in the office partakes heartily of a snack Wolfe has Fritz prepare for her Archie says "it is so agreeable to Wolfe to have someone enjoy food that he had almost forgiven her for losing control. He nearly smiled at her." Wolfe's prohibition against discussing business at the table is mentioned again, as is the following familiar activity: "Wolfe leaned back and closed his eyes, and his lips began to work, pushing out and then pulling in, out and in, out and in. He only does that when he has something substantial to churn around in his skull." When Wolfe is told that a man had apparently been converted to communism he says, "Then he's a jackass." Elsewhere he again uses the word jackassery. Finally, Wolfe gets kissed on both cheeks by his grateful female client. Archie does not record his reaction to this ordeal.

ARCHIE ::: "It is my habit, long established, when I open doors where I haven't been invited, to avoid touching the knob with my fingertips." This is the first time Archie has mentioned this habit. "I reported on my afternoon rounds, giving all conversation verbatim, which isn't so hard when you've had plenty of practice and have learned that nothing less will be acceptable." Wolfe gives Saul an assignment without letting Archie in on the secret.

OTHER REGULARS ::: Wolfe utilizes Saul's services and says that he "has extraordinary qualities and abilities," but Saul does not actually make an appearance in this episode. When Wolfe's clients want a lawyer Wolfe recommends Nathaniel Parker, but Parker does not appear, nor does Doc Vollmer, who is mentioned in passing by Archie. Archie talks to Lon Cohen on the phone, giving him an exclusive tip. Cramer and Purley both appear. We learn what Purley's voice is like: "His deep base was a little hoarse, as usual." Archie gives us a familiar description of Cramer: "a big husky guy with graying hair, a broad red face, and gray eyes." Cramer, incidentally, says that he knows Wolfe "won't take a murderer for a client knowingly." Rowcliff doesn't appear at all, though Archie mentions him: "I was hoping to be assigned to Lieutenant Rowcliff so I could try once more to make him mad enough to stutter."

PHYSICAL ASPECTS ::: The red leather chair "is roomy, with big arms", and the bookshelves in the office are mentioned again. We again learn that Archie's room has a private bath. The seven steps of the front stoop are mentioned again, as is the one-way panel in the front door. We are not given an address for the brownstone in this one, but we are told, indirectly, which side of 35th Street it is on when Wolfe remarks that "there is s back way out, leading to Thirty-fourth Street."

ROUTINE AT THE BROWNSTONE ::: The boys at the brownstone have gotten lax with the chain bolt again: "I let us in with my key, and, closing the door, shot the chain bolt." The doorbell answering question is becoming fuzzy again. After dinner Archie answers it because "Fritz was in the kitchen doing the dishes," which would seem to indicate that were Fritz not so occupied he would have done it. But elsewhere Archie answers the bell without hesitation and without mentioning Fritz. Lastly, "I seldom see Wolfe in the morning until eleven, when he comes down from the plant rooms."

ODDS AND ENDS ::: Only one, actually. Archie says, regarding the tip he gave to Lon from a phone booth, "If I had done it in the office Wolfe would have pulled his dignity on me and pretended to be outraged, though he knew as well as I did that it's always desirable to get your name in the paper provided it's not in the obituary column."

-"The Next Witness" [Summer 1954], published in *Three Witnesses*, 1956.

THE STORY ::: Two months earlier Leonard Ashe had tried to hire Wolfe to arrange with an answering service to have his wife's telephone conversations listened in on. Wolfe turned him down, because "I excluded from my field anything connected with marital difficulties." Ashe then proceeded to make the arrangements himself, and when the girl he was dealing with turns up strangled to death by a telephone cord at her switchboard with Ashe on the scene it isn't long before Ashe is arrested and placed on trial for the girl's murder. Wolfe and Archie are both subpoenaed as witnesses for the prosecution, and have to sit through the entire trial, which is going badly against Ashe. Suddenly, just before he is to be called to testify, Wolfe stalks from the courtroom. He explains his behavior to Archie thusly: "Soon I was going to be called as a witness, and my testimony would have been effective corroboration of [that of the chief prosecution witness]. It was intolerable. I believe that if Mr. Ashe is convicted of murder on the thesis Mr. Mandelbaum [the assistant DA] is presenting it will be a justicial transgression, and I will not be a party to it." Archie suggests that in fact Wolfe is motivated by the hope that if he gets Ashe off he will show his appreciation in some monetary fashion, and Wolfe doesn't deny it. Whatever his motives, Wolfe then proceeds to investigate the case vigorously, travelling hither and thither in a most unWolfean fashion and eventually gathering the information needed to clear Mr. Ashe. How he gets that information admitted into evidence—and incidentally keeps himself out of jail—is reminiscent of Erle Stanley Gardner at his best. Indeed, the entire episode, in court and out, begs comparison with the most outstanding of Gardner's Perry Mason productions. Wolfe does receive a gratuity for his efforts.

WOLFE ::: Of course, Wolfe leaves the brownstone in this one. In fact, he is never *in* the brownstone in this episode. What's more, he does an incredible amount of automobile riding by his own choice, both in New York City and out into Westchester county, and he converses extensively with Archie in a taxi, despite what has earlier been said of his inability to converse in an automobile. However, he "refuses to ride in front because when the crash comes the broken glass will carve him up." Since a warrant was issued for his arrest (and Archie's) when he wasn't in court when he was called to testify, he couldn't spend the night at the brownstone or he would have been picked up. So he and Archie spend the night at Saul's apartment. Saul's solution to the sleeping arrangements, Archie says, was to put "Wolfe in his bedroom [on Saul's only bed], me on the couch, and him on the floor." But for all this Wolfe has not overcome his distaste for leaving the brownstone--"He hated to leave his house at all, and particularly he hated to leave it for a trip to a witness-box." Bust since he *is* out he does a super job of investigating and quizzing on the scene, so to speak. For food while they are away from Fritz, "Wolfe and I . . . each disposed of three orders of chili con carne at a little dump on 170th Street where a guy named Dixie knows how to make it." Wolfe comes more closely into contact with people than he is used to doing behind his desk in the brownstone; "Wolfe backed up a step. He doesn't like anyone so close to him, especially a woman"; "I dislike conversing on my feet"; he gets patted on the shoulder and the top of the head by one woman; and in the middle of the court room another woman "threw her arms around his neck, and pressed her cheek against his," to which Wolfe's reaction is not recorded. Wolfe says "pfui", "autokinesis" and "contrariety", but he gets caught out for using imprecise language in court: "I allowed myself a grin. Wolfe, who always insisted on precision, who loved to ride others, especially me, for loose talk, and who certainly knew the rules of evidence, had been caught twice. I promised myself to find occasion later to comment on it." Archie says "Wolfe never missed a word of an account of a murder [in the papers], and his skull's filing system was even better than Saul Panzer's." Finally, Archie says "For his bulk he could move quicker and smoother than you would expect."

ARCHIE ::: Archie "was going to spend the evening at the Polo Grounds watching a ball game" before Wolfe decided to take it on the lam. That's it for this time.

OTHER REGULARS ::: Theodore and Lily Rowan are merely mentioned, and Fritz and Lon Cohen are only spoken to over the phone. We get just a glimpse at Purley Stebbins' back. Assistant D.A. Irving Mandelbaum, whose several earlier brief appearances I have not noted, prosecutes the case in this episode. He is "a little plump and a little short, bald in front and big-eared." But the person we learn the most about is Saul Panzer. First of all, Saul's apartment--on West 38th Street between Lexington and Third--has only one bed, and it is obviously a bachelor arrangement, which raises the intriguing question of what has happened to his wife and kids (who are not mentioned). What's more, Archie's remarks about poker in the following passage indicate that Saul's bachelorhood is of long standing: "Wolfe had never been at his place before, but I had, many times over the years, mostly on Saturday nights with three or four others for some friendly and ferocious poker. Inside, Wolfe stood and looked around. It was a big room, lighted with two floor lamps and two table lamps. One wall had windows, another was solid with books, and the other two had pictures and shelves that were cluttered with everything from chunks of minerals to walrus tusks. In the far corner was a grand piano. 'A good room,' Wolfe said. 'Satisfactory. I congratulate you.'" In the course of the evening Saul and

Wolfe play "three hot games of checkers, . . . all draws." Archie says "I suppose to some people Saul Panzer is just a little guy with a big nose who always seems to need a shave, but to others, including Wolfe and me, he's the best free-for-all operative that ever tailed a suspect."

PHYSICAL ASPECTS ::: Wolfe gives the address as 914 W. 35th St. The car [only one is mentioned] is a brown sedan and is kept at "the garage, on Thirty-sixth Street near Tenth Avenue."

ODDS AND ENDS ::: Archie says, "Our bank account needs a shot in the arm."

"Die Like a Dog" [late 1954 or early 1955], published in *Three Witnesses*, 1956.

THE STORY ::: When Richard Meegan tries to hire Wolfe to help him with his marital difficulties--his wife has run away from him--he is brusquely dismissed by Wolfe and grabs Archie's raincoat by mistake on his way out. Archie goes to return it, notices cops at the address, and comes away with the coats still unexchanged. While in the neighborhood a dog--apparently a stray--takes a liking to him and Archie takes him home to rag Wolfe before he turns him over to the ASPCA. Archie's joke backfires, however, and when it turns out that a man has been murdered in the house where Meegan lives Wolfe resolves to expose the killer, though his only client is the dog. An entertaining episode, and the essential clue is a good one, if a little obvious.

WOLFE ::: When Archie first appears with the dog (whose name, he tells Wolfe, is Nero) and pretends he wants to keep it--"You have your orchids, and Fritz has his turtle, and Theodore has his parakeets up in the potting room, and why shouldn't I have a dog?"--Wolfe, to Archie's great surprise, actually wants to keep it, though he transparently pretends otherwise: "I had learned something new about the big fat genius: he would enjoy having a dog around, provided he could blame it on me and so be free to beef when he felt like it." Archie doesn't like this, since he doesn't much care for keeping dogs in town, and he tries to weasel out, but Wolfe doesn't let him. Wolfe, who goes on to display considerable erudition on the subject of dogs, immediately recognizes this one as a Labrador retriever, and Archie says "I'm never surprised at a display of knowledge by a bird who reads as many books as Wolfe does." Wolfe muses about "a dog I had when I was a boy, in Montenegro, a small brown mongrel," while pretending indifference to the Lab. When Cramer shows up and wants to take the dog away for a police experiment regarding the murder Wolfe refuses on the pretext that he can no more let the dog be taken from the brownstone without a warrant than he could a human client, and in this way cunningly insures the dog's continued presence without having to admit that he actually *wants* to keep it. "Jet would be an acceptable name for that dog," he says with studied indifference. He eventually learns that the dog's name is really "Bootsie": "'Good Heavens,' Wolfe muttered. 'No other name?'" In the end Wolfe keeps the dog, who sleeps in the basement with Fritz, who is also much taken with him, and the regretable name Bootsie is dispensed with: "To relieve the minds of any of you who have the notion, which I understand is widespread, that it makes a dog neurotic to change his name, I might add that he responds to Jet now as if his mother had started calling him that before he had his eyes open." Though Wolfe's unexpected enthusiasm for dogs is the most outstanding item for this section this time out, there are other items as well. Wolfe's distaste for work regarding marital strife has been mentioned above: "I don't touch that kind of work. . . . My vanity bristles even at an offer of that sort of job." Archie mentions that "Mr. Wolfe dis-
-likes red

likes red. He likes yellow," and here's another example of Wolfe's distaste for upset women: "When something happens in that office to smash a woman's nerves, as it has more than onece, it usually falls to me to deal with it. . . . As for Wolfe, he skedaddled. If there is one thing on earth he absolutely will not be in a room with it is a woman in eruption." Still on the subject of women, Wolfe refers to one as "that volatile demirep." Here's a familiar item: "With his lips pursed, he was watching the tip of his fore finger make little circles on the desk blotter." No explanation of what it means this time. Here's another: "For Wolfe it was unthinkable to have company in the house at mealtime, no matter what his or her status was, without feeding him or her." In light of what Archie has said earlier about rarely seeing Wolfe before 11:00 a.m., this next item is unusual: "If you will come to my room before you go in the morning I may have a suggestion." Lastly, two of Wolfe's bad habits are in operation in this episode. One is familiar--he persists in the barbarism of dog-earing the pages of books--but the other is new: "Wolfe's voice came. 'Yes? Whom do you want?' I've told him a hundred times that's a hell of a way to answer the phone, but he's too damn pigheaded."

ARCHIE ::: Second mention of Archie's head gear--he wears "my old brown felt" out in the rain. Archie carries a gun we've not seen before, a Carley .38 [is this a typo, or is there such a thing?]. Archie -rinks some milk at one o'clock in the morning. Wolfe speaks of "Mr. Goodwin's admirable enterprise and characteristic good luck."

OTHER REGULARS ::: Cramer shows up: "His big round face was no redder than usual, his gray eyes no colder, his foice no gruffer. Merely normal." Archie says of him, "He does sometimes call me Archie, after all the years, but it's exceptional." Purley's around too" "Purley was half an inch taller than me and two inches broader." Saul gets mentioned, though he doesn't appear: "Saul is the best tailer alive." Fritz is present as usual, and he gives a woman "the look he gives any strange female who enters the house. There is always in his mind the possibility, however remote, that she will bewitch Wolfe into a mania for a mate."

PHYSICAL ASPECTS ::: The address is given as 918 W. 35th St., where it appears to have stabilized (within a few numbers). The coat rack in the hall is mentioned. On the floor in the office is "the best rug in the house, which was given to Wolfe years ago as a tiken of gratitude by an Armenian merchant who had got himself in a bad hole." "I went to the cabinet beneath the bookshelves, got out the Veblex camera, with accessories, slung the strap of the case over my shoulder . . . ."

ROUTINE AT THE BROWNSTONE ::: Archie answers the bell in this one. "It is understood that no visitor, and especially no officer of the law, is to be conducted to the office until Wolfe has been consulted." When Archie arrives home a little after six in the evening he lets himself in with his key, but when he gets home about midnight he has to ring the bell because the chain bolt is on. So, while the chain bolt appears to be used regularly at night as would be expected, the boys in the brownstone appear to have relaxed their vigilence while the sun shines.

MYSTERY*FILE

Short Reviews by Steve Lewis

A. S. Fleischman, *Shanghai Flame* (Gold Medal 181, 1951; 181 pp.).

    Time out for a history lesson. At the time of this story, Shanghai was settling down under the rule of the Communists from the surrounding countryside, and the pursuit of a not-so-ordinary pack of playing cards takes place across a city increasingly dangerous to be a foreigner in, much less an American. Whites were not yet a novelty, however, and displaced European refugees and all sorts of unsavory soldiers of fortune still played significant roles in the commerce and life of one of the Orient's most exotic cities.

    What Cloud does is to smuggle himself into Shanghai, hoping to regain the love of a woman he'd once walked out on, but in these surroundings all that it seems it will take is a single spark for the volatile romance to burn itself away in a spectacular flash of unrequited love. To the intrigue in which they find themselves securely entangled, add a deadline for being able to safely leave the city, Chinese pirates scouring the coastline, and the several sides of a labyrinthic doublecross, and you have the kind of book that's increasingly difficult to find these days when the whole world's but a step away--the pure adventure thriller written for the fun of it. (B)

Thom Racina, *Sweet Revenge* (Berkley 03559-X, 1977; 217 pp.).

    This was produced primarily for Baretta TV fans, although it does very effectively churn up plenty of emotions about the problems faced by law enforcement officers today.

    Apartment dwellers who'd rather not get involved, for example, even while watching a would-be rapist turn killer in a courtyard below. Or the ruin of a good cop, Tom Gumbar, tormented to extremes by a gang of young street punks determined to get revenge for his having sent one to jail. It could happen to anyone, for any reason, and there is no effective way of fighting back. You'll read this with clenched fists and teeth.

    The language is that of the streets, which is Tony Baretta's domain, but the treatment is shallow for the digging into society's problems that it pretends to do, and the ending suffers for it. Racina is, however, a good enough writer to suggest that he might do even better with his own characters. (C)

Sherman Williamson, *The Glory Game* (Walker, 1977; 189 pp.).

    Although isolated moments are very good, this is strictly minor league cloak-and-dagger stuff. It begins in Morocco, as an English girl escapes an unwanted marriage to a persistant emir, and leads to an in-depth tour of some of Europe's most notorious cities, hand-in-hand with a once-retired British agent who at first has his own purpose in mind. Only pieces of the puzzle are revealed at a time, and not quickly enough to keep disbelief from rapidly stealing in. (C)*

Lawrence Block, *The Sins of the Fathers* (Dell 7991, 1976; 189pp.)

    The title is a popular one. Without the "The", it's Ballantine's retitling of Ruth Rendell's *A New Lease of Death*, and with the "The", there's a recent science fiction novel by Stanley Schmidt. It's a good one for mysteries in general, and it says a little about the private

---

* Reviews so marked have appeared earlier in the *Hartford Courant*.

detective business in particular.

This is the first book appearance of Matt Scudder, ex-cop and unlicensed New York City private operative, and the title fits perfectly. Dead is a Greenwich Village prostitute, and also dead is the accused, her roommate, the homosexual son of a Brooklyn minister. Since he hanged himself in his cell, the police have closed the case, but the girl's father hires Scudder in a last attempt to learn to know the daughter he lost some time before.

Scudder's world is authentically rough and crude, not Miss Marple's corner of the universe at all, but surprisingly Scudder manages the same sensitivity to his fellow world inhabitants, belying the unnecessarily crass blurb on the back cover. (B)

James Patterson, *The Season of the Machete* (Ballantine 27105, 1977).

For reasons never made overly clear, the Mafia and the CIA combine forces to instigate a bloody revolution in the peaceful Caribbean island of San Dominica. Well, there are some indications of what it's all about, and it certainly is bloody, but this is not what you might call the entertainment of the year.

Piles of dismembered bodies grow as eye witness Peter Macdonald tries to tell someone he saw a blond Englishman near the scene of the first murder. It is not the black revolutionary Colonel Dred who's responsible, but the crack assassination team of Carrie and Damien Rose, and they seem to fear a double cross.

Although it's not very appealing, there is a sense in which this is a gripping story. The narration is heavy-handed, however; too much is revealed in advance and still there's nothing to clean up the mess afterward. (C plus)

Patricia Ponder, *Murder for Charity* (Manor 15281, 1977; 304 pp.).

Contradicting the ultra-macho image projected by the front cover, which shows the Cajun detective Louis Breaux being very protective of the cuddlesome Diana, this is in fact a detective story most reminiscent of the old-fashioned golden age of mystery fiction, complete with a country club overflowing with clues and suspects.

When Diana Parnell's aunt is murdered while she's running an antique show for charity, it's Diana who's suspected. The mysterious behavior of a friend caused her to be alone at the very moment for which an alibi is needed, but to here rescue comes Louis Breaux, convinced of her innocence even though they've only just met, and together they set off on the killer's trail.

It must be remembered that most of the books of the golden age have been forgotten, with good reason. Only the Christies and the Queens still survive, and they're still the models that other writers of pure detective fiction must strive to equal. Here's another that doesn't measure up. When the clues are as falsely represented or slighted over as they are here, it may be playing fair with the reader in a technical sense, but the edges of an otherwise pleasing performance are curdled.

Nevertheless, flaws and all, it was a nice surprise to find this. Mildly recommended for those who are nostalgic for this sort of thing. (C) [Note to bibliographers: Besides the haphazard proofreading system employed by Manor throughout the book, on the title page the author's name is given as Patricia Maxwell.]

Peter Way, *Dirty Tricks* (St. Martin's, 1977; 224 pp.).

According to the cover this is a novel of industrial intrigue and murder, while the implication of the back flap of the dust jacket is that it transcends the cardboard characters and the incredible events typical of the genre. I wouldn't know--I quit at page 24. For what it's worth: No rating.

Alex Gordon, *The Cypher* (Simon & Schuster, 1961; 252 pp.).

Some hero: a nervous, clumsy, asthmatic college history professor, unable to hold his own family together, unable to finish his life-long dream of cracking the cuneiform hieroglyphics of the ancient civilization of a country unnamed. That country still survives today, with a newly-formed government now friendly to the United States. What connection is there with the business code that Philip Hoag is asked to decipher by the uncle of one of his students?

There are undiscovered gems to be found in stacks of out-of-print mystery fiction, but this isn't one of them. Still, in a strangely naive way, it generates enough excitement peripherally related to the field of espionage, plus the slightest amount of detection, to warrant not being forgotten completely. (C plus)

Jonathan Stagge, *Death, My Darling Daughters* (Crime Club, 1945; 219pp.).

In cool, analytical fashion Stagge methodically bares the dabbling fraudulency that underlies the cultural legend pretended to by an ultra respectable New England family. The august Benjamine Hilton was once Vice President of the United States, and two generations later his family still finds delight in dropping names from the political and literary past. Their influence is used in hushing up the mysterious death of the family nanny during a secret scientific conference they are conducting, but their assumption that murder is beneath them is a disastrous one.

The unlikely investigator on the scene is Dr. Westlake, only physician for the small town of Kenmore, but this is not, however, the first case of murder he's had to deal with. Occasionally great Freudian profundities rear their ugly heads, but as a detective puzzle it's more than fair. Overall, an oversimplified view of life from another age. (C plus)

Anne Morice, *Scared to Death* (St. Martin's, 1977, US 1978; 192 pp.).

Major obligations on the part of an author are to introduce the characters as quickly and smoothly as possible, identify the relationships between them, and establish them in a situation intriguing enough to make the reader eager to discover how the problems are resolved. Morice fails in all respects. The reader is taken for granted, a bad mistake. Not even the "dying message" on page 61 could get me through this book. No rating.

Trevor Bernard, *Brightlight* (Manor 15278, 1977; 204 pp.).

Nathan Brightlight is a Hollywood private eye, working out of a corner of mystery fiction I usually turn cartwheels over. The wife of a fading movie star now consigned to a weekly television series has disappeared, and Brightlight is hired to find her, which of course involves considerable digging into the past.

Bernard is definitely not a word stylist of any shape or form. The terse, unimaginative commentary is embarrassing more than anything else, and it dies the lonesome death of a lame obligation. A third or fourth generation imitation, and yet . . . it involved me enough to read it in under two hours. Perhaps not completely hopeless? (C minus)

Brett Halliday, *Michael Shayne's Long Chance* (Dell 325, 1944; 192 pp.).

When the death of Mike Shayne's wife Phyllis has him packing up

shop in Miami, and ready to ca-1 it quits with his career as a private
detective, his old buddy, reporter Tim Rourke, with a nose for news and
an eye for a friend in trouble, starts him back on the right track with
a job that takes him back to the old stomping grounds he was once run
out of, New Orleans. And there, besides a nice girl or two to help
chase away the blues, he finds himself hip-deep in a case of murder,
complicated by police corruption and the dope-peddling racket in a city
where life can be loose and easy and more.

Shayne leads more with his head than he should, but he survives a
long night of beatings, doped drinks and a rigged picture frame to pull
off a decent bit of surprise trickery to nab the killer. The early
Shayne novels were not far removed from the the glory pages of *Black
Mask*, and this tale, no exception, goes down as smoothly as a bottle of
Monet cognac. (B)

Richard Sapir and Warren Murphy, *The Destroyer #31: The Head Men* (Pinnacle 40-153, 1977; 197 pp.).

Threatened in this, the latest adventure of Remo Williams and his
North Korean mentor Chiun, is the assassination of a newly elected
president who has a magnificent smile and comes from the South.

"So the President is going to be killed. So what?" Remo said.
"Have you seen the Vice President?" Smith asked.
"We've got to save the President," Remo said.

This particular president is a gutsy individual, who refuses to
spend his tenure in office as a prisoner inside the White House, but
of course that only makes the job harder. Sapir and Murphy have come
up with a neat theory of how presidents since Kennedy have avoided being assassinated, and their coarse comments on how affairs in Washington are conducted continue to cut across the grain of teeth-gritting
liberals, but there's no denying that the first half of this book is
much talkier than usual. Long-time fans of this series will be crying
for the action to start, and anyone else should find an earlier entry
and one more substantial to try their taste buds on. (C plus)

Elliot West, *The Killing Kind* (Houghton Mifflin, 1976; 231 pp.).

It starts fast, beginning just as private detective Jim Blaney
takes out two hoodlums seen shooting a pair of undercover cops, and
from that moment on events flow in a swirling multitude of directions:
a missing wife and some stolen diamonds, a raid on the home of a Las
Vagas casino owner, a daughter strung out on an overdose of heroin, a
$150,000 reward out the window when a client is murdered--or is it?

That's not all. Blaney has woman trouble as well, being happily
divorced and 30 years older than his secretary, who wouldn't at all
mind his moving in with her. He may have found the case he can retire
on, and if straddling the limits of the law will do it, well, maybe
it's worth the chance.

Two murders need a solution, however, and if there's a weakness
in the tale West tells, it's that it takes some questionable behavior
on Blaney's part before his deductions can be made to work--an objection outweighed in my mind by the many fine pages of character development and suspenseful action, with action the key ingredient of the mixture. (If you've come to think that I'm biased in favor of tough private eye yarns, I'd have to say you're right.) (A)

Robert Jagoda, *A Friend in Deed* (W.W. Norton, 1977; 212 pp.).

My advice, worth taking this time, is not to look at the blurb
inside the dust jacket flaps. As advertising executive John Storch
makes his magnificently elaborate preparations to kill his wife, you

know that by halfway through the book something crucial will have gone wrong, and I'm not going to tell you what, but I didn't let the plot be pre-summarized for me, and I'll tell you, I didn't have half a suspicion of what was in store.

Wasted words, I suppose. Everybody reads endflaps. You'll wish you hadn't, though.

The only common interest that Storch and his wife have in common is--no, make that three: the two national pastimes (one's baseball and the other isn't) and their dog, a poodle named Friend. (Animal lovers, here's a mystery for you.) She's otherwise obnoxious (the wife, that is), and rich, and so she has to go. A basically repugnant idea, and the second half is much better.

Quietly hilarious, and very sexy. Once on the right track, of course I had the solution before Storch, but I'm afraid I found that the ending aroused too many disquieting moral quibbles for me to be wholly satisfied. (B plus)

Jack Foxx, *Dead Run* (Bobbs-Merrill, 1975; 176 pp.).

Honest work in Singapore having become scarce since his recent affair with the jade figurine, Dan Connell takes a job as overseer of a rubber plantation in Malaysia's Selangor province, but the trip up the coast by slow steamer leads him into more trouble and adventure than even a man of Connell's unsavory past has a right to expect. Two men are seen throwing overboard a third man, a fired bank employee who had stopped briefly in Connell's cabin, but quickly it becomes obvious that they were frustrated in getting from him what they wanted. There's a girl, too, the plantation owner's daughter, with whom Connell ends up lost in a leech-infested jungle, and a hair-raising airplane flight with a madman lovingly caressing a grenade ready to go off at any minute.

The plot ingredients are easily recognized as those of countless plup adventure thrillers, but they are by no means outdated, as Foxx/Pronzini capably shows. It's reassuring to learn that there are still places in this world far enough away for the special flavor of the exotic unknown to be kept alive, capable of giving the reader that intimate thrill of escaping into another world of romantic adventure. Indeed, this has the same immediacy as that provided by the urgent voice-over narration of a top-notch radio drama. The early dialogue may seem stilted, but as the full artillery is let loose, the theater of the reader's mind will have that pair of deadly killers breathing down his or her very own neck. What more can you ask? (A minus)

George Bagby, *The Original Carcase* (Crime Club, 1946; 221 pp.).

Time out for a lesson in the antique furinture business. First of all, the word carcase--a more elegant word for carcass--has the meaning you think it has, but it's also the large bottom cupboard space found in antique dining-room sideboards. Of course, it's also true that if certain partitions were removed, there'd be room enough to stuff a corpse for safe-keeping, and so it happens, to the newly-wed neighbors of George Bagby. That the husband's brother is a retired gangster of no little repute, and known for a long time by Bagby's friend Inspector Schmidt, is also worth pointing out.

There never was a night like this in the old days, as even the old bootlegger is forced to admit, and as morning arrives, another killing occurs, and things get even goofier for a while. Schmitty is never at a loss for theories, however, and a final round-up of the suspects leads to a climactic solution scene that lasts for all of twenty-five pages.

Except for an unexplained lapse on the part of one of the characters, which makes him an unwitting accomplice of the real killer, this is really a fine example of how the light touch can liven up the serious business of police work--as long as it's the events that amuse rather than characters that are utterly wacky. (B minus)

Patricia Moyes, *Black Widower* (Penguin, 1975, 1977; 221 pp.).
When the racy Lady Ironmonger, wife of the new Tampican ambassador to the United States, promises to become a distinct political liability to her husband's career, it occurs to someone that murder can sometimes become a necessity. It's a long way to Scotland Yard from the Georgetown section of this nation's capital, but since Tampica is a newly independent British colony, the fie minutes of delicate diplomatic maneuvering that it takes to get Chief Inspector Henry Tibbett involved are easily managed.
A deal for a U.S. naval base on the island turns out to be quite important, and with the scene jumping back and forth between Washington in springtime and the breath-taking vistas of the Caribbean, one looks forward with anticipation to the eventual unravelling of all the little secrets that the staff of a minor embassy can possess. However, Moyes seems to be greatly out of her depth working with a motive depending so greatly on high finance and international politics. The feeling is overwhelming that she'd feel much more at home with the domestic malice of the "body in the library" sort of tale. Some characters, never well defined, remain murky to the end, and with such an obvious clue as to the killer's identity, I can only say I wasn't overly impressed. (C+)

Willard E. Hawkins, *The Cowled Menace* (Sears, 1930; 313 pp.).
If I were to guess, I'd say you're thinking "Ku Klux Klan" right about now, but, no, instead of the white sheets of racial intolerance, the cowled menace of this early detective story is that of monkshood, the wild flower whose poisonous brew has become a traditional part of the legend of Theseus and Medea.
Yes, a detective story, told in that glorious but supremely artificial style of the Golden Age of detective stories. Doing the sleuthwork is the famous Balmore O'Day, criminologist, investigator extraordinary, complete with a less brilliant assistant named Gillespie, who tells the story of how, in spite of three eye-witnesses, a man is cleared of murdering the husband of the woman he loves.
Its naive simplicity is about as far from today's police procedurals as can be imagined, and it takes place in a timeless world of never-was that yet could be yesterday, or 50 years ago. At times tinged with the purplish prose of Gothic terror, and utterly hopeless as a document of social significance, nevertheless this only mystery novel of Willard Hawkins still provides an evening's worth of entertainment. It never promised more than that. (C minus)

Michael Butterworth, *Remains to be Seen* (Crime Club, 1976; 185 pp.).
Two minor bureaucrats in an obscure Washington office, to justify their salaries not to mention their jobs, start in motion a chain of unlikely events that brings the close attention of several world powers down upon the British descendants of a Russian prince who escaped the Bolsheviks two generations before. That two of Davydov's sons, now named Davis, are undertakers is quite crucial to the plot and to the success that the third son, a dreamer and a fourth-rate poet, has in finally finding himself and quite rightly rising to the occasion.
With some quick shuffling of a dead body or two (you knew?) and a hi-de-do comic routine as minor everyday problems escalate out of

control. Butterworth entertains without ever producing real in-the-aisle laughter, lacking the spark of truly insane genius that would set the affair out of the ordinary. (C plus)

Donald MacKenzie, *Raven and the Kamikaze* (Houghton Mifflin, 1977, 190pp)
When Raven's roguish friend Count Zaleski drunkenly denounces a fellow exile as a member of the KGB, he unwittingly disrupts the man's delecate plans for a final act of revenge aimed at the Russians, setting off a race against time to find the desperate man before he destroys his unknown target.
Since retiring from Scotland Yard as a detective inspector, Raven has had several exciting adventures worthy of print, but while this affair has all the right ingredients--spies, counterspies, and a beautiful woman in love with the hunted man--it seems to rush headlong and downhill into an ending which comes as a total letdown. (C plus)

Patrick Alexander, *Death of a Thin-Skinned Animal* (Dutton, 1976; 231pp).
In the world of politics, the strangest bedfellows can suddenly become the most expedient allies. Case in point--two years ago Richard Abbott was sent on an assassination mission, to eliminate an unwanted African dictator. Now, after being betrayed, imprisoned and abandoned, when he manages to excape, he finds his target an honored guest back in England. For reasons of oil and uranium, it has become the task of his colleagues in British Intelligence to stop him, at all costs.
The plot structure is based on some rather questionable actions and non-actions, but Alexander otherwise has such masterful control over some very human characters, who live, love and die as real people, that it seems unfair and quarrelsome to even bring it up. (A minus)

John Lutz, *Bonegrinder* (G. P. Putnam's Sons, 1977; 254 pp.).
We're all afraid of the dark, why not admit it? It's only after you've tucked yourself in your own particular sanctuary against the night that it becomes safe to snuggle up with this kind of book, one designed to send chills running up and down spines, about a bone-crushing monster which suddenly emerges from nowhere to begin terrorizing the over grown wilderness of the Ozark lake country.
As much emphasis is placed on the disrupted lives of the local residents and the strange behavior of the irresistibly drawn tourists as on the unknown menace which threatens them, seldom seen but never far from anyone's thoughts. Is it science fiction? Lutz is a detective story writer also, and so while there is a tendency to expect him to come up with a rational explanation, he manages to keep doubts tantilizingly alive long in anticipation of the final chapter. A first-rate job of story-telling. (A)

Lawrence Block, *Burglars Can't Be Choosers* (Random House, 1977; 177pp).
Meet Bernie Rhodenbarr, a true professional with a feeling for his work--burglary. He thinks he knows all the angles, but on a routine breaking-and-entering accepted on assignment, he's caught in the act, with a corpse (unknown to him) in the bedroom. A little detective work is in order--who set him up and why?
Block's light and easy style will get you through a couple of chapters at a time with no effort at all. Even though the ending seems elaborately overbuilt, there's no danger of it collapsing to spoil the entertainment. I particularly enjoyed the similarities pointed out between sex and successful burglary--tickling all the right tumblers, slipping in a little at a time--as opposed to the smash-and-grab sort of approach. (B)

VERDICTS

(More Reviews)

Dorothy B. Hughes, *Erle Stanley Gardner: The Case of the Real Perry Mason* (Morrow, 1978; $15.00; 350 pp.).

    Erle Stanley Gardner seemed to be born a combatant, with a boundless zest for competition and an unstoppable drive to succeed. In 1899, at the age of ten, he wrote a school essay retelling the Greek myth of Atalanta, with its theme that whoever does not win the race dies. As a teenager he boxed for money, and later was expelled from college for slugging a professor. But as a flamboyant California trial lawyer he found a form of combat at which he could excel, and as the author of hundreds of pulp magazine stories and as the creator of the world's best-known fictional attorney, Perry Mason, he hammered out an imaginative universe which made him a megamillionaire. His books contain few literary graces but boil over with excitement thanks to his sheer raw storytelling skill, breakneck pacing, corkscrew plots, fireworks displays of courtroom tactics (many based on gimmicks he used in his own law practice) and his dialogue, each line of which is a thrust in a complex ritual of oral combat.

    At his publisher's request mystery writer Dorothy B. Hughes, who is still fondly remembered for her suspense novels of the 1940s, has written what is billed as Gardner's biography. Her book touches all of the familiar bases, evoking Gardner's youthful brushes with the authorities, his unorthodox California legal practice, the long years he spent grinding out a pulp novelette every three nights while lawyering full-time during the day, and the 1933 breakthrough into fame and wealth with the creation of Perry Mason. We learn of ESG's factory-like work methods which allowed him to produce torrents of words streaming from his dictaphone, of his fabulous Temecula rancho, his journeys of exploration into the wilderness areas he loved so deeply, the founding of the Court of Last Resort to free wrongfully convicted prisoners, the launching of the Mason TV series, and the final but still fruitful years before his death of cancer in 1970. A substantially complete checklist of Gardner's literary output, including those hundreds of pulp yarns, is printed as an appendix.

    Hughes' book is smoothly readable as a summation of Gardner's life and character and beliefs, but it's not quite a biography, since most of the text consists of letters to and from Gardner interspersed with ESG's dictated autobiographical statements. Hughes has filled out these materials with letters and reminiscences from surviving members of Gardner's personal and professional "family", but in an unseemly paroxysm of modesty she has let ESG speak for himself almost without interruption, so that of her own view on Gardner as a mystery writer and as a man we learn next to nothing. Even when Gardner's letters are hopelessly cryptic, and he discusses without identifying a crime novel by himself or a competitor, Hughes doesn't bother to give us the title in question. And her own habit of abandoning chronological sequence every so often without clearly signaling to the reader causes us to lose the threads of a developing life and body of work.

    It remains for some tireless researcher of the future to provide a judicious assessment of Erle Stanley Gardner. But that person will owe much to Dorothy B. Hughes for this hard-to-pidgeonhole book that is neither a biography nor an autobiography nor a collection of letters but, like the horseman who rode off madly in all directions, tries to be everywhere at once. (Francis M. Nevins, Jr., from the St. Louis

Globe-Democrat).

Jon Tuska, *The Detective in Hollywood* (Doubleday, 1978; $14.95; 436pp.).
The detective has dominated American popular fiction and films of this century more than any other mythical figure except the cowboy. Beginning in the late 1920s, a small army of deductive geniuses marched into print and public acclaim, among them such outstanding characters as Philo Vance, Ellery Queen and Nero Wolfe. Despite individual differences all of these master detectives were portrayed as brilliant, dynamic, eccentric intellectuals, or in other words as American variants of Sherlock Holmes. But during the same period there emerged a new and fundamentally American embodiment of the detective figure--the private eye. Tough, cynical, unloving and unloved, aware of the corruption all around him and at times more than a little corrupt himself, the private investigator was no more realistic a figure than the Holmes-like amateurs he sought to replace; but Dashiell Hammett, Raymond Chandler and dozens of lesser-known "hardboiled" writers opened up the detective story to bleak visions of the world that were inconceivable within the rational and optimistic framework of the clues-and-deductions school.

Both types of American detective have been translated again and again into film. Philo Vance, Charlie Chan and a host of other supersleuths cracked crimes with effortless ease for the enjoyment of moviegoers during the Thirties, while the characteristic detective films of succeeding decades were the darkly hypnotic private eye epics from *The Maltese Falcon* (1941), starring Humphrey Bogart and directed by John Huston, to *Chinatown* (1974) in which Jack Nicholson played the private eye and Huston his adversary. In *The Detective in Hollywood* Jon Tuska has set himself the triply ambitious task of writing a history of the American detective film, an account of the lives and fictional worlds of various mystery writers whose detectives were transposed to the screen, and brief sketches of some of the directors and scriptwriters and actors who helped bring the detectives to cinematic life. In eleven lengthy chapters he covers the Sherlock Holmes phenomenon, the life and times of S. S. Van Dine and his influential detective character Philo Vance, a potpourri of 1930s cine-sleuths (including Nero Wolfe, Bulldog Drummond and Perry Mason), the screen adventures of Charlie Chan and other Oriental detectives, the career of Dashiell Hammett and the film lives of his private eyes, an assortment of movie series from the Forties (The Saint, The Falcon, The Crime Doctor, The Whistler), the Hollywood experiences of Raymond Chandler, the genre of *film noir*, and a rather hurried survey of the current scene in detective films.

Unfortunately the book suffers from disorganization, awkward jumps from Hollywood's golden age to the present and back again, a compulsion to show that Tuska is on a first-name basis with the movie people he has interviewed, the inclusion of several sections that don't belong (like the material on the Agatha Christie-based Miss Marple films, which weren't even made in America), and the disinterest in a number of films that needed more attention (like Robert Aldrich's 1955 *noir* masterpiece *Kiss Me Deadly*). Solemn yet passionately enthusiastic, copiously researched yet marred by several avoidable factual slips, *The Detective in Hollywood* is a sprawling, quirky, informative and fascinating look at how the mystery film moved from the cozy world of the supersleuth to the grim universe of the private eye. Flaws and all, it belongs on the shelves of crime buff and cinephile alike. (Francis M. Nevins, Jr., from the St. Louis *Globe-Democrat*).

Joe Gores, *Gone, No Forwarding* (Random House, 1978; $6.95; 201 pp.).

Among the countless mystery writers who have published private eye stories, only two of any consequence have actually worked for a detective agency before writing. The first was the legendary Dashiell Hammett, whose tales of The Continental Op and Sam Spade revolutionized the mystery genre in the late 1920s. The second is Joe Gores, who like Hammitt writes of a San Francisco agency in a lean spare prose and with hard knowing eyes.

In his third novel about Daniel Kearny Associates, the agency has to fight an attempt by the state of California to lift its license on charges that seem to have been trumped up by state functionaries in collusion with organized crime. Kearny sends out two key operatives--the cocky womanizer Larry Ballard and the shrewd black ex-boxer Bart Heslip--on a cross-country search for the missing witnesses who may save the agency, while he himself and his feisty little lawyer Hec Tranquillini face a courtroom-like administrative hearing rife with perjured testimony. The license proceeding soon becomes intertwined with a recent mob execution in which the person identified by an eyewitness as the hit man has a perfect alibi provided by Kearney's own agency, and some brutal buddies who are preparing to maim and kill in order to keep that alibi unbroken.

In this taut, explosive, irresistibly readable private eye procedural, as we watch operatives running down leads to missing people we are shown a prodigious variety of high and low lifestyles, from the super-rich through the middle-level bureaucracy to the world of gays and gypsies and street blacks. The action-crammed final scene is too precisely choreographed to be credible and some of the plot details can't survive a backward look, but for readers willing to suspend their critical faculties Gores offers a heart-stopping roller-coaster ride through six major cities and a gallery of people at every social level, all observed with Hammett-like clarity and precision. (Francis M. Nevins, Jr., from the St. Louis *Globe-Democrat*).

Eric Ambler, *A Coffin for Dimitrios* (Del Mar: Publisher's Inc./University Extension, University of California at San Diego, 1978; $5.95; 264 pp. Introduction by Elleston Trevor, annotated bibliography by James Sandoe, illustrations by Karl Nicholason. Originally published by Hodder and Stoughton in 1939 as *The Mask of Dimitrios* and by Knopf in the same year under the above title.).

The sixth Mystery Library is precedent-setting in two ways. From the earlier selections, one would have thought that the Mystery Library board was comprised of a group of closet necrophiliacs, worshiping only dead authors; but here is a novel by an author not only living, but still active, with his last novel out just last year. Second, the TML people have entered a new field, although we shall soon see that this spy novel is not quite what it would seem.

We begin in Istanbul in the seedy days of the late Thirties. Charles Latimer is a university professor turned detective novelist, whose works range from *The Gettha Programme of 1875* to the very Farceur-sounding *"I", Said the Fly*. While at a party, Latimer meets Colonel Haki, of the Turkish secret police. Haki tells Latimer the story of Dimitrios Makropoulos, whose sordid career included what would seem to be every known vice wanted by Europeans, and a few that were unknown. Latimer, intrigued by Haki's story, resolves to find out more about Dimitrios, and thus begins a search that leads him to question officials and criminals across Europe. Aided by the enigmatic Mr. Peters, Latimer comes across information that would be worth a good deal of money--if he would abandon his values and sacrifice his honor. Latimer eventually learns the true story of Dimitrios—only at the cost of discovering what his values meant in a decaying world.

It should be clear from the description that this is not a spy novel. It is, rather, a detective novel about spies, and while this difference may seem minor, it is all the difference in the world. Nearly all the action is offstage; Latimer's job is to detect, not conflict with, the shadows of the past. Managing such a feat is difficult for any writer, but Ambler manages to pull it off through the search for the past and the constant interest in Dimitrios's shady world. It all seems rather quaint in a way—who worries about white slavery and the munitions makers in these days of global terrorism and the neutron bomb? Nevertheless, Ambler manages to capture the essence of a time superbly; the Thirties still speak to the Seventies, if only we listen to what Ambler has to say.

While the novel is highly and enthusiastically recommended, this edition, sad to say, is not. The Mystery Library has always had a bad habit of surrounding good authors with bad criticism, and that unseemly tradition continues here. Elleston Trevor's introduction is an amiable chat about Ambler, although one wishes that Trevor would spend more time discussing the novel in question. He is, however, preceded by an extremely fatuous introduction by John Ball, who wastes two pages on how great Ambler is, how great Elleston Trevor is, and how privileged we all are to read such a great book written by all these great men. One wonders if Ball would have bothered with this exercise in bathos if Michael Gilbert, originally scheduled for this book, had written the introduction. There are also reprinted essays by the unreadable Ronald Ambrosetti and the wrongheaded Gavin Lambert, as well as stills from various Ambler movies. The most pathetic section, though, is by James Sandoe, an alleged checklist that is easily the worst article yet in this series. Sandoe does such things as omit Ambler's screenplay for the movie of Geoffrey Household's *A Rough Shoot*, think "Belgrade 1926" to be a short story when it was actually the chapter of that name from this novel (reprinted in John Welcome's *Spies and More Spies*, published by Faber and Faber), and forget the English title of *The Siege of the Villa Lipp* (*Send No More Roses*)—and those are only the minor errors. Sandoe also omits *any* detail about publishers and does not bother listing the sequel to *The Light of Day*, *Dirty Story* (published in 1967). In his time, Sandoe did much to advance the state of mystery criticism, but his day is past, and it would be best for him to retire on his well-deserved laurels, instead of trying to pretend that he is still a master of the bibliographical art. (Story A, Appendices D)   (Martin Morse Wooster)

Ellery Queen, *The Tragedy of X* (Del Mar: Publisher's Inc./University Extension, University of California at San Diego, 1978; $6.95; 297 pp. With Introduction and Checklist by Francis M. Nevins, Jr., illustrations by Joyce Kitchell. Originally published by Viking and Cassell in 1932 as by Barnaby Ross.).

The seventh Mystery Library book continues the admirable trend of publishing authors that are still living. I need not introduce Queen to any of you; Frederic Dannay and Manfred Lee were perhaps the greatest collaborators in detective fiction, and Dannay still continues an admirable career as editor and raconteur to-day, seven years after the death of his cousin.

For reasons known only to themselves, the Mystery Library cartel has chosen to reprint, not a novel featuring Ellery Queen, but one from Queen's other series, the quartet featuring Drury Lane, retired Shakespearian turned amateur detective. The choice, as we shall see, was not unfortunate.

The plot centers around Harvey Longstreet, stockbroker and manipulator of millions. One night, after a drunken party, Longstreet boards the local trolley, where he is killed by a cork laced with poison needles that the murderer stuck in Longstreet's pocket. Anyone on the trolly could have killed Longstreet, so the New York police, led by the oddly named Inspector Thumm, have their work cut out for them. Thumm diligently questions subjects and sifts through clues, until Lane (in the grand manner) announces that he knows who the murderer is, but will not tell Thumm as he does not have enough evidence to convict. Lane then proceeds to manipulate the other characters, occasionally helping and frequently hindering both the police and the suspects; at one point, he even disguises himself as Thumm to gather evidence. After several other murders, and much movement via train and ferry (which, as a fan of those two modes of transportation, pleased me a great deal) murderer and motive are revealed in thirty pages of thorough deduction. (This time, I guessed wrong on both the murder and the motive.)

This is an excellent example of the classical (or "Golden Age") detective story, the sort that plays fair with the reader and whose plot is intellectual instead of visceral. Queen, however, tried to provide their [I can hardly address two writers in the singular. Thus, when I refer to Queen as "they", I mean Lee and Dannay; "he" is a reference to Dannay alone.] detective with psychological depth; instead of pursuing justice, Drury Lane pursues power, manipulating the characters so that they can adjust their roles and emotions to fit the requirements of the theater. To satiate this power-lust, Lane constantly witholds evidence, conducts illegal searches, lets the police knowingly arrest the wrong person so that Lane can give to the defense attorney vital exculpatory evidence, and so on. Lane is the only character in the book that possesses more than two dimensions, and these depths only come across when Queen is not being "psychological"; that is, when Lane discusses the theater, or dying messages, or asks for information. Queen tried too much here; their ambition exceeded their skill, and the novel is successful only as a traditional detective novel, not, as Nevins would have it, "a disturbing study of power . . . a superb portrait of a time and a place." (Nevins's statement elsewhere in his introduction that Nietzsche would have loved the book strikes me as being an extraordinarily fatuous statement from one of the more competent critics in the field.)

The appendicies are good, though not superior. Nevin's introduction, despite his tendencies towards unnecessary praise, is a thorough review of Queen and his work. Queen himself contributes a short Letter to the Reader, giving much interesting and pertinent information. There are also some contemporary reviews of the book, a photo of the original jacked (with the original artist uncredited), a photo and map of the Third Avenue trolley provided by Berenice Abbott, a conscientious New York City reader, and a profile of Queen from a 1967 MD, with the profiler, again, uncredited. (I hope he or she was paid for reprinting the story.)

My chief criticism of the appendices is with Nevinss's checklist of Queen works. Ellery Queen provides many challenges for the bibliographer, as there are no less than four categories of spurious Queen works. First, there are the juveniles as by Ellery Queen, Jr. (eg, *The Golden Eagle Mystery*, Stokes, 1942). Second, the novelizations written about the same time, which I have not seen, although I have heard of such titles as *Ellery Queen, Master Detective*. The third and fourth such categories both deal with sixties novels; there are the series of paperback originals featuring Paul Corrigan, the superspy with the eye-patch, as well as non-series books, including *A Study in Terror*; these, I am told, were all written by Paul Fairman. Then there are the "legitimate" Queen novels possibly written by other hands; rumor has it that *The Player on the Other Side* was written by Theodore Sturgeon and *And on the Eighth Day* by Avram Davidson. Nevins tries to clear up some of these problems by only listing those novels he considers legitimate; but while he disowns the Barnaby Ross historicals (actually written by Gardner F. Fox, prince of hacks) he nonetheless leaves *The Player on the Other Side* and *And on the Eighth Day* in, as well as the highly questionable *A Study in Terror*; thus the problem of authorship grows murkier and murkier. Perhaps the next time you pick up an Ellery Queen novel, you should ask yourself, not "Whodunit?" but "Who wrote it?" (Story A-, Appendices B+) (Martin Morse Wooster)

Isaac Asimov, *Asimov's Sherlockian Limericks* (Mysterious Press, 1978; 60 pp.; $7.50, $20.00 for limited edition).

In one of the Black Widowers stories (I forget which) a character mentions doing a series of 24 limericks based on the *Illiad*, one for each book of that epic. I suspect Penzler read the same story and encouraged Asimov to write this extremely short book of sixty limericks, one for each story of the Canon. Asimov has written three books of "lecherous limericks" (which aren't very lecherous) and judged a national limerick contest, so one would expect him to be a master of the form. And so he is; the book is very good in a technical sense. But the spirit of the Canon is, understandably, lacking; although one admires Asimov for accomplishing a feat, one remains puzzled at why anyone would *want* to summarize a novel in five lines. I would much rather have Asimov return to the jingly, Gilbert-and-Sullivanian poetry he wrote in the fifties; a book of longer poems by Asimov on Sherlockian themes would be worth having, while this mistake can only be recommended for the fanatical Asimov reader or the hyper-fanatical Sherlockian. (Martin Morse Wooster)

Richard Hull, *A Matter of Nerves* (Collins, 1950).

Richard Hull was one of the most interesting crime novelists working, usually, in the inverted form in the 30's. His first and best novel *The Murder of My Aunt* (1934) is regarded as a classic.

Hull, along with many other mystery writers, suffered a period of literary inactivity during World War Two. After hostilities ceased, Hull returned to the scene with 6 novels published between 1946 and 1953.

Alas, the spark was gone. The acid bite and inventiveness were replaced by sheer unpleasantness and, all too often, tedium. None were published in America, and they sank into the oblivion that most of them seemed to deserve. (I except *The Martineau Murders* [1953] which I have not read from the above remarks.)

Possibly *A Matter of Nerves* is the best of this group--if only for its "stunt" which I believe is original. Otherwise, it's only fair. It gets a bit dull in the middle, but does manage to accelerate as it moves toward its inexorable conclusion.

It's set in the small and well-limned East Anglian village of Losfield End, and purports to be the diary of one of the inhabitants. It opens just after the narrator has committed what he hopes to be the perfect crime: the murder of local butcher John Hannan. He sets the scene to look like an accident, but a stupid mistake combined with a nervous reaction obviates that possibility, and he is forced to dispose of the body--in sections.

The narrator continues to tell the story of the events leading up to the crime, and its aftermath.

Rumors among the townspeople concerning Hannan's disappearance are eventually dispersed when the police recover the victim's remains, and a full-scale inquiry follows. All the while, the events and the reactions of the individual villagers--including those of the narrator--are faithfully recorded in the diary.

Hull's ingenuity consists of the narrator's refusal to reveal his identity. Obviously, the diary, if placed in the wrong hands, can be damning evidence.

The narrator records events and conversations in which he has participated, but will only refer to himself in the third person. He takes literary license and reconstructs where he was not present, and, of course, does not differentiate.

The ending of most stories told in the inverted form is predictable. In *A Matter of Nerves* the narrator does manage to drop a few clues that enable Scotland Yard's Inspector Morrison (and possibly the alert reader) to discover his identity before the diary is concluded. (Charles Shibuk)

Clifford Witting, *Let X Be the Murderer* (Hodder, 1947).

The *Encyclopedia of Mystery and Detection* is obviously guilty of widespread errors of omission. One major author who has been neglected here--and in most of the other standard reference works (with the honorable exception of *A Catalogue of Crime*)--is Clifford Witting.

This British author wrote 16 detective novels of varying quality between his debut in 1937 and his final work (to date) in 1964. Only one of these novels, *There Was a Crooked Man* (1960), was published in America--by the British Book Centre in 1962. However, somehow or other, I did manage to stumble across a copy of the inverior *Villainous Saltpetre* (1962) in a local library.

Witting dod not start well as a detective novelist, but improved as he gained experience. His masterpiece *Measure for Murder* (1941) as well as *Subject--Murder* (1945), *A Bullet for Rhino* (1950), and *There Was a Crooked Man* are worthy of the most serious attention.

Let X Be the Murderer is an excellent work, and I would rank it slightly below *Measure for Murder* and *Subject--Murder*. *X* does not have the gripping early sections of its predecessors, but it is a smoother and stylistically more even piece of work.

It is lightly written, but mostly serious in tone, and moves steadily and agreeably forward from first page to last--with the notable exception of an unnecessary four or five page recapitulation of the crime given at midpoint by series character Detective-Inspector Harry Charlton of the Lulverton C.I.D. to his superior officer Superintendent "Tiny" Kingsley.

X commences when elderly manufacturer Sir Victor Warringham calls police headquarters to complain that he has been attacked in the middle of the night, while in bed, by a pair of luminous hands.

Charlton attempts to visit Sir Victor, but is refused admission by relatives. So, too, is Sir Victor's legal advisor. Hints of mental instability are bruited about, but a few questions in the right quarters by Charlton uncovers a possible plot directed against the wealthy Sir Victor.

An unexpected development occurs that same evening when murder strikes--not against Sir Victor, but his housekeeper.

Police investigation uncovers some interesting clues, and a small but lively group of well-characterized suspects--most of whom are possessors of many less than admirable traits.

Charlton's efforts, aided by Detective-Sergeant Bert Martin and Detective-Constable Peter Bradfield (who will be featured in subsequent Witting novels), are brief, but painstaking and thorough, and the investigation is concluded in 2 days.

X is not a major example of *fair play* detection, and, at times, comes perilously close to the police procedural form, but it does contain some nice misdirection, and a neat triple-twist climax. (Charles Shibuk)

John Spain, *Death Is Like That* (Dutton, 1943; Popular Library 178, 1949).

"Spain" was a pseudonym of Cleve F. Adams, a popular L.A. hardboiled writer of the forties who is largely forgotten today. This book is one of his very best.

Hero Bill Rye is a trouble shooter for millionaire Ed Callahan. Callahan once saved Rye's life (we're never told just how) and there is a far deeper bond running between the two than mere employer/employee.

Callahan owns the Governor of California. However, it's election time and the campaign is a bitter, underhanded one. The candidate opposing Callahan's man is owned by a ruthless newspaper magnate who would like nothing better than to dig up a juicy scandal on either Callahan or the Governor to smear across the front pages of his dailies and shoo his own man into office. Since Callahan's family is comprised of a promiscuous alcoholic wife, a short-tempered, hell-raising son and an ex-showgirl daughter-in-law who still years on occasion for the fast life, Rye, needless to say, more than has his hands full.

If the Rye/Callahan relationship and the casual acceptance of all-pervasive political corruption reminds one of Hammett's *The Glass Key* at times, Adams was nonetheless a supremely gifted original talent and *Death Is Like That* is a tough guy masterpiece of intricate plotting, non-stop pace, colorful characterization, incisive wit and a writing style evocative of Chandler at his best ("Across the hall someone must have told a funny story. The shrill laughter of women topped the deeper tones of men like the froth on beer.").

A hard one to find, but well worth the effort to any fan of the hardboiled genre. (Stephen Mertz)

Peter Cheyney, *You Can't Keep the Change* (Collins, 1940; Dodd, 1944).

Peter Cheyney was an Englishman who produced 33 novels and countless short stories and novelettes between 1936 and his death in 1950. His specialty was ersatz hardboiled "American" thrillers aimed at Britishers and Europeans, although he eventually acquired a considerable following in the U.S. as well. His attempts at American tough guy dialogue are uniformly, unintentionally hilarious--far closer to Damon Runyon than Dashiell Hammett--yet he was immensely popular and in 1944 sold more than one and a half million copies of his novels worldwide. He was the Carter Brown of his day, most of his books streamlined affairs, topheavy with dialogue and double entendre, written with a decided glint in the eye, meant to pass a few hours leisure reading time and nothing more.

This one stars Slim Callaghan, London private eye, and is representative. Someone has broken into Margraud Manor and made off with the ancient family jewels of Major Vendayne. Slim and his comic-relief partner, Canadian Windemere "Windy" Nikolls, are called in and things immediately begin popping at such a pace that Callaghan and Nikolls barely have time to keep up with their considerable boozing and oggling of the ladies. The case involves the Major's three lovely, headstrong daughters and plenty of assorted hoods and blackmailers, and includes some well done atmospheric renderings of the seedy nightlife of wartime London.

Cheyney's strong points were pace and plotting and this one scores high on both counts. Callaghan is an active, aggressive protagonist and the tale moves so swiftly that the plot's minor holes and flaws barely register until well past the final page. In addition, there is a well-executed last minute twist that is both unexpected and legitimate.

Cheyney was a man of his time, though, and his work is crude and dated by today's standards. Still, readers with an interest in what Hammett's and Chandeler's contemporary imitators were up to across the Atlantic will find this a fascinating oddity of the hardboiled school. (Stephen Mertz)

Jack S. Scott, *Shallow Grave* (Harper & Row, 1977; $7.95).

Following the murder of a young schoolmistress in a small English village policemen and reporters descend upon the town and it soon is evident that the late Miss Beavis was not quite what she pretended to be. The police are hampered in their investigation by mutual hostility between the two leading policemen, and by their frantic desire to do something--anything--to solve the case without suffering the indignity of having to call upon Scotland Yard for assistance. The Chief Superintendant, though competent, is afflicted with arrogance, snobbery and throughout this case, a severe case of the trots, which sharply curtails his freedom of movement. He intensely dislikes his immediate subordinate, upon whom he looks down, and stands ready to dump all the blame on him should the investigation be less than successful. This subordinate, Detective Inspector Rosher, is, in fact, a rather unpleasant chap, and he reciprocates his superior's disliking in full measure. He is also suffering from pre-retirement blues and from frustration resulting from the fact that the buxom publican's wife for whom he has the hots obviously has her eye set on Rosher's own subordinate, young Sergeant Cruse, who is damned near the only wholesome one in the bunch.

Scott populates his novel with strongly drawn characters such as these. He is not the first mystery writer to portray his principal detective (Rosher) in a thoroughly unpleasant light. Joyce Porter's Dover, for example, is so extravagantly gross that, perversely, it's a joy to read about him. But where Dover, from his total lack of redeeming qualities, is not really believable, Rosher, whose foibles and frustrations have understandable roots, must be dealt with as a person rather than just a caricature. Indeed, it is Scott's unusual technique of showing the reader the causes of his characters' unpleasantnesses that is the real strength of the story. One may laugh at Dover with a clear conscience. One may also laugh at Rosher, but the laughter of all but the most callous will be tinged with sadness and pity. (Guy M. Townsend)

Richard Himmell, *The Twenty-third Web* (Random House; $8.95; 309 pp.), C. A. Haddad, *Operation Apricot* (Harper & Row; $7.95; 179 pp.).

Two novels of intrigue were added recently to the growing roster of books about the Middle East. Both deal with a planned destruction of Israel, one from within the country, one from abroad.

The Twenty-third Web marks the hard-cover debut of Richard Himmell, who presents a frightening premise: terrorists spin a web of blackmail and murder around the rich supporters of Israel in the United States, entangling them in a maze of shameful secrets, concealed vulnerabilities, clandestine relationships.

Among their targets are a prominent banker who has an extramarital affair with a young girl; a macho symbol of a merchandising conglomerate who is closeted in a homosexual relationship; and a mousy Irish servant girl who inherited the fortune of her Jewish husband, and then used it to buy the sexual services of countless young men.

The plot is somewhat too complicated, with American, Russian, Israeli and Arab agents chasing one another in a vicious circle, but there is a chilling drive to the narrative, and one is impelled to turn the pages until the final outcome.

There are numerous sequences with graphic sex descriptions that would place the book in an X category.

Operation Apricot by C. A. Haddad features the humorous, tongue-in-cheek, James Bondish adventures of David Haham, an Israeli ex-intelligence officer who embodies the story of his people--wanderings, turmoil, oppression, struggle and ultimate triumph.

Haham was born in Iraq, where his Jewish family had been murdered. He escaped to Israel, where he was put in an immigrants' camp, and later was placed in the home of a sadistic uncle. Eventually he became a successful, powerful business man.

An easy prey to the charms of the fair sex, Haham is enticed by a lovely lady reporter to investigate a conspiracy against the Israeli government. Shortly thereafter he finds himself at odds with the Shin Bet--Israel's domestic security unit--with the Prime Minister, the American Ambassador, all leading to a climactic life-or-death clash with Arab terrorists in Southern Lebanon.

This is Haddad's third novel of suspense. The publishers refrain from printing any biographical data about him. However, his tart style, the picturesque locales, the zany illogical plot twists and the uniquely arrogant sense of humor are indicative of the sharp ironic pen of a Sabre, an Israeli born writer.

There was a time when Sax Rohmer, the creator of Fu Manchu, wrote imaginative fantasies about Egypt and Agatha Christie wrote a series of old-fashioned detective stories utilizing an excavation background in Palestine, Jordan and Iraq. These yarns belong to another era. Nowadays, suspense fiction featuring the Middle East, provides not only thrills and entertainment, but also reflects the modes of the times, as so ably evidenced in *The Twenty-third Web* and *Operation Apricot*. (Amnon Kabatchnik)

Les Daniels, *The Black Castle* (Scribner's; $8.95;241 pp.), Basil Copper, *The Werewolf* (St. Martin's Press; $8.95; 240 pp.).

Bar the windows, latch the shutters, seal all doors. The horror tale is in vogue again.

Perhaps it is due to the enormous success of the revival of *Dracula* on Broadway, or the box-office bonanza of movies like *Jaws*, *The Exorcist* and *The Omen*. Or possibly it follows the best-selling status of *The Amityville Horror*.

The fact is, enterprising publishers are bombarding the literary market with a continuous barrage of spine-tingling tales stamped with supernatural phenomena.

The modern horror story does not jeopardize the classical stature of Mary Shelley's *Frankenstein*, Robert Louis Stevenson's "Dr. Jekyl and Mr. Hyde", Bram Stoker's *Dracula*, H. G. Wells' *The Invisible Man* and Edgar Allan Poe's masterful short stories of the macabre.

Still, there are a few new interesting entries in the genre, fiction and non-fiction.

The Black Castle by Les Daniels combines a winged vampire with a beautiful witch, the Grand Inquisition and an ancestral castle in Spain of 1496.

It is the story of two brothers, whose fortunes are ensnared in a web of evil. One of them is the Grand Inquisitor of a remote region, and his pious hypocricy masks a lust for power. The other has become a living dead, a vampire, hiding in a black castle that looms over the terror-stricken town.

While the plot progresses with a relentless drive, but few surprises, the main strength of the narrative is in evoking a chilling picture of Spain engulfed by the horrors of the Inquisition. There is a particularly ghoulish scene, not for the squeamish, in which the torture methods of the era are graphically described.

The Werwolf by Basil Copper covers in fascinating detail the myth of Lycanthropy--the gradual change of man into wolf.

The study deals with the legends that made the monster one of the most feared of beings. In ancient times it was believed that Lycanthropy was an actual physical state in which men became transformed at the full of the moon, then rampaged and destroyed anyone unfortunate enough to wander into their path.

During medieval times thousands of suspected werewolves were destroyed in judicial holocausts.

There is a touching chapter in the book about feral children, wolf-boys and girls reared in primitive circumstances by the beasts of the forest.

Then there is a detailed analysis of the treatment of the werewolf in literature (distinguished works by Frederick Marryat, Alexander Dumas, George Reynolds, Guy Endore, Ambrose Bierce and "Saki", among others) and on the silver screen (notably *The Wolf Man* starring Lon Chaney, Jr., 1941, and *The Curse of the Werewolf* featuring Oliver Reed, 1961). (Ammon Kabatchnik)

Ross Macdonald, *Lew Archer, Private Investigator* (The Mysterious Press; $10.00; 245 pp.), John D. MacDonald, *One Fearful Yellow Eye* (Lippincott; $8.95; 286 pp.).

Lew Archer and Travis McGee, the most famous private detectives in contemporary literature, are back.

Lew Archer, Private Investigator is the first complete collection of short stories featuring the hard-boiled, synical and lonely dick. The only previous volume dedicated to some of Archer's short exploits was *The Name Is Archer*, a paperback original published in 1955 by Bantam.

Graced with a new introduction by the author, this new, handsome book presents Archer as a probing private eye who gets entangled in complex mysteries across Southern California.

The finding of a pint of blood in a motel room, a charcoal sketch of a nude female with a thick beard, a $5,000 bank withdrawal, a lost overseas cable are some of the instigating catalysts that draw Archer into a maze of grim and deadly cases.

But his involvement and sleuthing are not dictated by the traditional gathering of clues. He has an insatiable interest in other people's lives, often transcending his own interests. Many of his adventures begin with chance acquaintanceships.

As created by Ros Macdonald, Lew Archer was a policeman in Long Beach, California, until he was fired because he would not work under a corrupt police administration. He became a private investigator. His marriage has fallen casualty to his work as his wife, Sue, "didn't like the company I kept." Largely autobiographical, Archer, like Macdonald, is sympathetic to the plight of the young and is committed to fight those who would despoil the environment.

Short stories evidently served as the laboratory from which emerged one of the few mystery writers also regarded as a major American novelist. Written between 1946 and 1965 for various magazines, the stories lack the depth and texture of Macdonald's later and longer works, but are still widely interesting, peppered with vivid prose and numerous surprises. The characters are drawn sharply with a metalic pen, especially the femailes of the species.

Travis McGee, created by John D. MacDonald, is another modern knight-errant. He lives on a boat in Fort Lauderdale, but his deep loyalty to friends compells him to leave Florida for the big cities. In *One Fearful Yellow Eye* he journeys to Chicago to aid a former girl friend whose husband was defrauded of $600,000 before his death.

Travis finds in winter-dismal Chicago a nasty case of blackmail and encounters a sadistic murderer. Before the final conclusion he utilizes all his physical and mental resources to stay alive.

John D. MacDonald is probably more renowned than any other writer of paperback originals. His narrative abilities have gained him considerable praise. Richard Condon called him "the great American storyteller. Anthony Boucher described him as "the John O'Hara of the crime-suspense story."

While most paperbacks are reprints of the hard-cover edition, John D. MacDonald's works go through a reverse publishing phenomenon [*until recently*]: His original paperbacks are now being published by J. B. Lippincott Company in hard-cover. It is a testimonial to his near classic standing among whodunit followers.

So both Lew Archer and Travis McGee, big, strong, rough and scrupulous, are back again to thrill legions of readers. Like their predecessors Sam Spade and Philip Marlowe, they are steadfastly becoming cult figures. (Amnon Kabatchnik)

THE DOCUMENTS IN THE CASE
(Letters)

From David Doerrer, 4626 Baywood Circle, Pensacola, FL 32504:
If you are back on schedule, [Ha!] this is going to be too late for
2:4, but I wanted to send something more than my last excuse. ¶ I received my copy on May 26 with no postage visable and the "First Class
Mail" statement crossed out. Did you send it first or second class?
[Yes.] Is the application for second class an attempt to hold the line
on the subscription rate? ¶ Put my big foot into mouth of equal size
in passing on John McAleer's offer, didn't I. I re-read his letter to
be sure I hadn't goofed, and that's what he said, honest. When John
reads TMF 2:3 he'll no doubt advise our friend in the black T-shirt
that there was a chap in Massachusetts using the name McAleer, but he's
now living in Florida under the name Doerrer. I'll have to stop leaving the drapes open after dark and oil my Belgian Browning 9mm, if I
can only remember where I put the shells .... ¶ While we're on
this topic, i.e. *Rex Stout: A Biography*, I hope none of TMF's readers
were put off by Julian Symons' review in the *Times Book Review*. I
haven't read it, but Bill Crider reports in TAD 11:2 that it is highly
unfavorable. I've just finished reading *Rex*, and I'm inclined to disagree with Symons even if I don't know what I'm disagreeing with! I
found the book well-written, tremendously interesting and balanced.
It is certainly the best biography I've read. ¶ The chap who assembled TMF 2:3 after the editor's unfortunate demise must have failed to
check the stencils. My copy was missing page A6, the continuation of
the interesting cover article. I was particularly intrigued by the
reference to Demosthenes, whose unfortunate demise was reported in an
earlier issue of TMF. (That got a bit thick, didn't it? Well, my 6th
grade teacher told me that she found my sense of humor peculiar.) ¶
On the continuing debate over the number of reviews versus letters, I
personally like the present mixture. I'm always amused by Jeff Banks'
deprecations of l-o-c's, which invariably precede his own tremendously
interesting comments. If the letters were all nothing more than "I-like-this, I-didn't-like-that", then I too would agree that the space
could be better used, but I think that those of us who don't know as
much about the field as some of the old hands find as much of interest
in the letters as in the articles. My own order of reading each issue
of TMF is Table of Contents, "Mysteriously Speaking", "Documents", the
Saga, the reviews and last the articles. ¶ Concerning the Saga, I'll
hate to see it end, but I'd like a promise that you won't pull an *Edwin
Drood* on the rest of us Nero Wolfe fans. [*Considering why Dickens never completed Drood, I'm afraid I can't promise that the same inconvenience won't prevent me from completing the Saga. But, barring that
eventuality, I have every intention of completing it in its present
form and then re-writing it for book publication. I have, in fact, already written several publishers about it, though the response has all
been negative so far. I'll persist, though, and print it myself, if
necessary.*] ¶ A naive query, if you'll permit. Where do you and the
other regular contributors find the time for all the research and writing? You do work, don't you? Or are you all as fortunate as Jeff
Banks, who apparently can combine his vocation and avocation into one?
¶ On the letters in 2:3. As one who found fault with one of Myrtis
Broset's reviews, I'm very glad that she wasn't so discouraged that she
quit. A reviewer's opinion and/or interpretation of a book may add or
detract from the value of the review for the reader. If I find myself

in regular disagreement with these, I'll stop using his reviews as a guide to my reading. (I agree that English needs another pronoun, but I'm having enough trouble trying to produce error-free copy without trying to remember to use his/her, etc..!) A factual error, however, disturbs me because I don't know if it is a one-time slip or a warning flag that the reviewer has only skimmed the book. If the latter is true, then I dan't trust other reviews of books I haven't read. This is a long preamble to the fact that I feel an obligation to point out factual errors if I find them. I certainly didn't intend my comment as a put-down, but I can't accept the implication that "non-professional" status excuses one from responsibility for descriptive accuracy. (I don't want to start an acrimonious debate, Guy, so if you think this subject is better left closed with your editorial remarks, feel free to omit all the above.) [*Far be it from me to stand in the way of an acrimonious debate.*] ¶ I for one would be most interested in an article on collecting if Steven A. Stilwell would do one. ¶ Joe Lansdale has a very good point when he says that "not having to account for one's actions . . . is what causes crime, not the media." What the media (TV) is doing in what appears to be an attempt to produce violence-free crime them programs to placate the anti-violence PTA vigilantes is abominable. If anyone had the misfortune to see the pilot for an alleged espionage series called "Escapade", you know what I mean. I'm no champion of gratuitous violence (or sex) for its own sake, but I resent the attempts of any self-appointed censors to prevent anyone from seeing--and the next step is from reading--anything they object to because they've abdicated their personal responsibility for monitoring what *their* children see. ¶ I have to second Bob Briney's plea for full bibliographic data, including series, when citing books reviewed. This latter element is crucial in building checklists, tracking down variant editions, etc., especially in paperback publishing. I know that Berkley reissued seven (at least) of Richard Stark's (Donald Westlake) Parker novels in their series The Violent World of Parker; I'm looking at the books, but you won't find them in *Book Publishing Record*. ¶ This particular example, plus a number of similar frustrating experiences, plus Jay Broeckner's request for checklists, leads me to ask: would there be any interest out there for a collection of checklists? This would require the help, and permission to reprint, of those who have already done the hard work of compiling them, but I'll stick my neck out and offer to do the reproducing and distribution at a cost which would recoup my out-of-pocket expenses. ¶ I'd also like to see the Joe Gall chart. In fact, I'd like to see it strongly enough, Guy, that I'll volunteer to type it if you'll provide me with those "exacting specifications". (This reckless penchant for volunteering dates back to my Basic Training days when I volunteered to be a "fireman" and discovered that this meant learning how to keep the coal furnace going while my fellow troops were out shoveling snow!) ¶ I'm dubious about Bob Adey's preference for TMF's current format because he sees it as easier to bind. I think the margins, judging from 2:2 and 2:3 are too slim; you'd get a very tight volume. The margins of 2:1, which he had in hand when he wrote, were considerably wider. Of course, if he is planning to do his own hand binding, that's another matter, as he could control the amount of trimming. Those who are contemplating binding their issues of TMF might be interested in Rigby Graham's "Bookbinding with Human Skin", *The Private Library*, vol. 6, January, 1965, pp. 14-18. ¶ Did Judith Fiene really find Geri Frazier's comments hard to *bare*? If not, and it was only a typo in transcription, I hope Sandy Sandulo offers another of her interpretations! I'm really a lousy proof-reader; hate to go over something I've written, and would never have made it through graduate school without my wife's eagle eye. Consequently, I usually read right through someone else's errors without seeing them, but if you can promise me inspired ones like these each issue I'll watch for them. ¶ The Tiger Mann chart was interesting to me as I hadn't realized that the series had been such a short one. I've read only one--I think it was *Day of the Guns*--years ago and it left me unimpressed, as did the later Mike Hammer books. ¶ Stephen Mertz didn't convince me that Carroll John Daly was either a better writer or more influential than Dashiell Hammett, but that is because I've read nothing of the former's work; a situation Mertz has convinced me I should correct. I'd like to see a critique of the TV version of *The Dain Curse* in a future issue of TMF. I'm not going to attempt it because I don't feel qualified to make a critical evaluation. I will say that I found the spot scenes for the second and third parts almost as irritating as the seemingly innumerable commercials. ¶ Not including the *Saga*--which I think is in a class by itself--I most enjoyed Marvin Lachman's Gideon Fell article. I'd like to try something similar on Stark's Parker novels--unless someone tells me it's already been done--but I haven't been able to get my hands on all the titles. If some kind soul out there can help me fill in the gaps . . . . In the meantime, I'm enclosing a preliminary bibliography consisting of all titles and variant editions which I have been able to verify to date. If anyone can supply additions and/or corrections, please don't hesitate to do so. I'll welcome these almost as much as finding the titles I lack. ¶ Did you hold George Kelley's article on "The Caper Novels of Tony Kenrick" because of lack of space? I was looking forward to it because I've read *The Chicago Girl* and found it rather uneven and unconvincing in parts. [*It's in this issue.*]

[*I'm printing David's preliminary bibliography of the novels of Richard Stark below in hopes that TMF's readers will be able to fill the gaps, thus enabling David to do a definitive article on Parker for TMF in the near future. Here it is.*]

*The Blackbird. New York: Macmillan, 1969. (A Cock Robin Mystery); Toronto: Collier-Macmillan, 1969. (A Cock Robin Mystery); London: Hodder, 1970.

The Black Ice Score. Greenwich, Conn.: Fawcett, 1968. (GM Book D1949); New York: Berkley, 1973. (The Violent World of Parker, no. 3).

*Butcher's Moon. New York: Random House, 1974.

+The Dame. New York: Macmillan, 1969. (A Cock Robin Mystery); London: Hodder, 1969.

+The Damsel. New York: Macmillan, 1967; London: Hodder & Stoughton, 1968. (King Crime); New York: NAL, 1969. (A Signet Book P3874).

Deadly Edge. New York: Random House, 1971; New York: Berkley, 1974. (The Violent World of Parker, no. 7).

The Green Eagle Score. Greenwich, Conn.: Fawcett, 1967. (GM Book d1861); London: Hodder/Fawcett, 1968. (Coronet Books).

The Handle. New York: Pocket Books, 1966. (Later edition has title: *Run Lethal*.)

The Hunter. New York: Pocket Books, 1963, copyright 1962. (Permabook edition M-4272). (Later edition has title: *Point Blank*.)

*The Jugger. New York: Pocket Books, 1965. (50149). (Later edition has title: *Made in U.S.A.*)

Killtown. New York: Berkley, 1973. (The Violent World of Parker, no. 5). (Earlier edition has title: *The Score*.)

*+Lemons Never Lie. New York: World, 1971. (A Falcon's Head suspense novel.)

*Made in U.S.A. ? ? ? (Earlier edition has title: *The Jugger*.)

    The Man with the Getaway Face. ? ? , 1963.
    **The Mourner.* ? ? , 1963.
    The Outfit. New York: Berkley, 1973, copyright 1963. (The Violent World of Parker, no. 4.)
    **Plunder Squad.* New York: Random House, 1972.
    Point Blank. Greenwich, Conn.: Fawcett, 1967. (GM Book D1856); New York: Berkley, 1973. (The Violent World of Parker, no. 2). (Earlier edition has title: *The Hunter*.)
    **The Rare Coin Score.* Greenwich, Conn.: Fawcett, 1967. (GM Book D1803); London: Hodder/Fawcett, 1968. (Coronet Books.)
    Run Lethal. New York: Berkley, 1973. (The Violent World of Parker, no. 6.) (Earlier edition has title: *The Handle*.)
    The Score. ? ? , 1964. (Later edition has title: *Killtown*.)
    The Seventh. New York: Pocket Books, 1966. (50244) (Later editions have title: *The Split*.)
    Slayground. New York: Random House, 1971; New York: Berkley, 1973. (The Violent World of Parker, no. 1.)
    The Sour Lemon Score. Greenwich, Conn.: Fawcett, 1969. (GM Book R2037); London: Hodder, 1973. (Gold Lion Book.)
    The Split. Greenwich, Conn.: Fawcett, 1966. (GM Book D1997); London: Hodder, 1973. (Earlier edition has title: *The Seventh*.)
    The Steel Hit. ? ? ?
+ = titles with Alan Grofield rather than Parker as the main character. I've included these because Grofield is a character in some of the Parker books and vice bersa.
* = titles I lack.
From George Kelley's comment on the Coronet series in TMF 1:5, I assume that Hodder/Fawcett did more than the two titles I have listed, but these were all I have been able to verify so far.
[*God, how I hate typing these damned things!*]

    From Robert E. Briney, 4 Forest Avenue, Salem, Massachusetts 01970: I guess I'd better say something about TMF 2:3 before any more time passes. It is a fine issue--that goes without saying--with outstanding contributions from Marv Lachman, E. F. Bleiler, yourself, and Steve Lewis. The latter's reviews keep getting better all the time, and I hope they will remain a staple of TMF. (Sometime I must find out when Steve finds all that time for reading . . . .) ¶ You may not like this suggestion, but: if lack of "traditional" artwork leads to the use of items such as this issue's cover then perhaps the artists in the audience should continue to be chary with their contributions. Otherwise we might be deprived of some welcome and enjoyable humor. ¶ My favorite item this time is Marv Lachman's survey of the career of Gideon Fell. It is valuable for its arrangement of the cases in order of internal chronology and for the tracing of the Carr-surrogate persona through the series, as well as for the acute observation and enjoyable prose which mark all of Marv's work. ¶ E. F. Bleiler's article on European books about mystery fiction gives me some new items to track down. European (and other non-English) attitudes and perceptions need to be better known than they are, and commentaries like Blieler's--and, one hopes, Helmut Masser's promised article--perform a valuable service. ¶ There are at least three other recent French books on the genre which are worth attention. My favorite is Francis Lacassin's two-volume *Mythologie du Roman Policier* (Paris: Union Générale d'Editions, 1974; #867 and #868 in the collection "10-18"). Sixteen chapters on individual authors or detective characters, with detailed bibliographies and filmographies: Poe, Holmes, Leblanc, Father Brown, the Lone Wolf, Charlie Chan, Hammett, Pierre Véry, William Irish, Chandler,

Jean-Louis Bouquet, Kenneth Fearing, Fredric Brown, Boileau-Narcejac, and Chester Himes. *Le Roman Policier* by Josée Dupuy (Paris: Librairie Larousse, 1974; in the collection "Textes pour Aujourd'hui") is a textbook which comes across as pretty much of a hodge-podge: extracts from novels and stories, none more than a few pages in length, surrounded by annotations, short essays, lists, outlines, and even some schematic diagrams of plot structures. Possibly a systematic reading would find more in it than my hasty examination has done. Thomas Narcejac's *Une Machine a Lire: Le Roman Policier* (Paris: Denoël/Gonthier, 1975; #124 in the collection "Bibliothèque Médiations") is a philosophical and psychological analysis of the classic detective story, centering mainly around the works of R. Austin Freeman, Ellery Queen, John Dickson Carr, Agatha Christie, and G. K. Chesterton. The book is larded with annotated quotations from Boucher, Haycraft, Nicholas Blake, and many other commentators on mystery fiction. ¶ A recent issue of *The Bookseller* reveals a pen-name that was new to me. "Michael Sinclair", author of *Vorslag*, *The Dollar Covenant*, and other novels, turns out to be Michael Shea, current press secretary to H. M. Queen Elizabeth. The same issue mentioned a film version of Erskine Childers' *The Riddle of the Sands*, currently being made, with Michael York, Jenny Agutter, and Alan Badel. (Does anyone remember Badel in "The Stranger Left No Card", one of the finest mystery movies ever made?) ¶ Re: Jay Broecker's request for a checklist of the Pyramid "Green Door" mysteries, you will have seen by now that the second issue of *Paperback Quarterly* contains just such a list, prepared by Howard Waterhouse. The same issue contains an advertisement for checklists of Ace, Avon, Dell, Popular Library, and Armed Services Editions paperbacks (through 1959 only). Maybe I'll try one of them, and if it looks well done I'll get the others as well.

From Jeff Banks, Box 3007 SFA Station, Nacogdoches, Texas 75962:
Here it is the last day for the 13¢ letter and I'm using it to write you an l.o.c. on the latest MFr. I, for one, liked this cover fine, tho it is the kind of joke that will work on a particular audience only once. I wonder howmany readers noticed that the headline just below the "mysterious" news item was a Nero Wolfe allusion? ¶ And speaking of Wolfe, I wish you had used some of the 20 pages you devoted to letters--and, as with every protest against letters, I include mine as one that could have well been dropped, even though it was obviously written for publication--for more of the Wolfe Saga. ¶ Also, speaking of close and careful reading, as I was in the first paragraph, I wonder how many caught your beautiful joke (or was it a poetically apt slip-up) [*I wonder if it is a Sin to let people think that certain typos are intentional . . . .*] about your own "musspellings" in the midst of your sermon on careful MS. preparation (p.68). ¶ I'm glad you ran the Tiger Mann chart, and I enjoyed (and approve of) the sentiments in your response to that portion of my letter which referred to it. Spillane in having Mann question the loyalty of the C.I.A. was reflecting the 1950s opinion of the Birch society and other far right groups who, at least that long ago, could not accept the more obvious explanation for our frighteningly consistent foreign policy that would blame all mistakes on stupidity. The Birch version was that the old O.S.S. (from which the C.I.A. was eventually formed) had been so riddled with Communists in WWII that MacArthur had refused to allow it to operate in the Pacific Theater; furthermore, they were told to believe that the real reason for HST's removal of MacArthur was to allow the C.I.A. to operate in the Far East, as he (MacArthur) was still roadblocking it there during the Korean thing. In light of the performance of recent U.S. Presidents, the stupidity explanation makes

lots more sense. ¶ Enjoyed Joe Lansdale's letter and your response, and even the continuation of the response in your comments on the letter which followed it too. The last real FAN letter that I wrote Al Hubin concerned an issue of TAD (2 or 3 before the format change) that had an unaccustomedly high ratio of humorous content. This latest issue of MFr does too, and I believe that if we can't laugh at ourselves and each other we should all change hobbies. ¶ I continue to delight in Steve Lewis's review column. It is (for my money) your best continuing feature. He's put me onto more good reading I'd have otherwise missed than any other single reviewer. And many of the treasures he's pointed me toward have been early Gold Medal books of the kind he had an extensive aside about in this issue. However, as usual, I'm going to disagree with him about some of what he has to say. In a column reviewing 21 books (I think, and I'm not going to count them again), he includes 4 reviews of private eye books (my favorite kind), but in the Chastain review remarks that such books are almost never written/published anymore. His own column, and the ratio of 5 out of 16 private eye books covered by your other reviewers, I think proves that he is wrong. I certainly do agree, however, that there aren't nearly enough books of that sort appearing these days. ¶ Steve Mertz's defense of Daly was my favorite article in this issue. By extension, it is also a defense of Spillane, and that's something I feel like I've been doing singlehandedly for years. Sometime back, Steve mentioned to me that he was contemplating an article for you on "the Spillane citcle"--Dave Gerrity, Charlie Wells and that group. I hope he hasn't dropped that very worthy project! [*Steve?*] As I mentioned last time, Parker was a speaker at the recent Pop Culture Assn. meeting. I was quite impressed by him and recorded his speech, though the quality of my recording is too poor to share it with others. (I was learning to use some new equipment. ¶ Now, to the delight of my Celtic ancestors, I'm going to close this in order to get it off in time to save 2¢. But, before I do, I must add that I enjoyed all the rest of your latest issue, even though I did not comment individually on several items. You have a good group of contributors. Last of all, no George Kelley this time; I hope he'll be back in your next!

From Jeffrey Meyerson, 50 First Place, Brooklyn, NY 11231:
I enjoyed the latest TMF once the P.O. got done crumpling it a bit on a rainy day. Cover was amusing, though of course nothing less would be acceptable from reviewer of *Beak!*, right? ¶ Marv Lachman's article on Fell was absolutely great. I especially liked the way he pointed out the use of Carr surrogates, and how they aged at the same rate as their author. I am looking forward to further entries in this promised series, but if I had a vote I'd go for other than the proposed Campion (covered in TAD) and Wolfe (done by you). How about Nigel Strangeways or Judge Dee, just to name a couple of possibilities? Of course I'll take what I can get. ¶ Since I have only read 2 or 3 stories (and no novels) by Carroll John Daly I wouldn't presume to judge him at this point. However, if he is as good as Steve Mertz says wouldn't some of his gooks have survived to the present day? Even one? I don't like Spillane, but his books are certainly available. If Daly is so good I can't help but believe something of his would be available somewhere, other than the single story Steve mentions (which I thought was soso-- fast moving I suppose, but unmemorable). Hammett needs no defense from me, so I'll forego one. ¶ Since you keep telling everyone that I'm an expert on English book-buying I thought I better say a few words before I'm deluged with requests. I know London best, naturally, and have found many good, cheap books in the various small used bookstores

along Charing Cross Road. You can try Joseph Poole, Albert Jackson & Son, E. Joseph, Collet's Penguin Bookshop, but no guarantees. Otherwise Foyle's (further up Charing Cross) has a large selection of hardcover mysteries, including many reprints. The recently opened (last fall) Alamo (Shepherd Market, Mayfair) supposedly stocks every title currently in print, but I won't be able to verify that till after the summer. Outside of London I've found books as far afield as York, Wells, Salisbury, and Edinburgh, just by walking around looking for shops. Again, I should be able to provide more concrete information later this year. Hay-on-Wye (border of Wales) is supposed to be an entire town made up of bookshops! Sounds like paradise. ¶ A friend of mine visited the *New York Times* with his junior high school class and took the opportunity to ask his guide if it was true that Newgate Callendar was really music critic Harold Schonberg. He was told, "We're not supposed to reveal that information." ¶ That Kenneth Millar half-hour on PBS was incredibly boring; he read from his works in a monotone, nothing of interest. On the other hand, P. D. James on Dick Cavett's show was delightful. And Dick wasn't as flippantly obnoxious as usual. She spoke about her books and series detective Adam Dalgleish, as well as her background, etc. It seems her children didn't think her first book could be much good since it was accepted immediately, as everyone knows that all good writers can paper their walls with rejection slips!

From Martin Morse Wooster, 2108 Seminary Rd., Silver Spring, MD 20910: It's good to see TMF after so long. I was especially pleased by the comments by Stephen Mertz, an author I highly respect. He has rescued me from my months of inactivity and got me interested and active in the field again, after months of lethargy. [. . .] ¶ I am thinking very seriously about starting a fanzine for historical novels. This is a field that I feel has never been explored. I would like to see, though, if there is any interest in such a zine among TMF readers, and what, if anything, the readership would be willing to contribute. (Please, though, do *not* send me contributions. Just suggestions.) Depending on the response, I should have a prospectus in a few months. ¶ And speaking of historicals--would you be interested in an article on George MacDonald Fraser? I finished *Flashman's Lady* a while back, and feel compelled to write about it and Fraser. I'm not sure if an article about him would be in scope for TMF, so I thought it would be best to ask, knowing your interest in history. [*I do have an interest in history and I have been a Fraser fan ever since the first Flashman book appeared (though I'm having the damnedest time wading through the latest), but space limitations keep me from including anything non-mysterious in these pages. Thanks anyway, and good luck with the historical fiction fanzine; I, for one, am quite interested.*] [*. . .*] ¶ On to TMF. I can see why Bob Adey had a hard time trying to find out about Maarten Maartens. Maarten Maartens was a pseudonym of Josua Swartz-- or, at least, this is what the Library of Congress claims. It seems that Wood had nothing to do with *The Black Box Murder*, save for the mistaken heading by the reprint publisher. I should assure both these gentlemen that there is a copy of the book in the Library of Congress, and I would be happy to provide photostats of the title page and the verso if they request it. (Indeed, I will do this for any TMF reader who needs to verify the existence of a book or needs other bibliographic information. I do ask that they provede a SASA with their requests.) ¶ Stephen Mertz does a good job in arguing for the merits of Daly, but he is wrong when he says that Dashiel Hammett wrote *Red Harvest*, *The Maltese Falcon*, and *The Glass Key* after leaving the pulps. At least two of those novels were serialised in *Black Mask*, and possibly all three. Shouldn't Mertz have said that Hammett left the pulps and wrote *The Thin Man*? ¶ As for the proper form for citations, you are quite right when you argue for minimal description. There are, however, some times when more detail is necessary. I use a complete citation when reviewing Mystery Library books because the readers should know who is listed on the title page, as it is of some importance to know which portions of the critical material the editor felt were worthy of mention. And an extremely short description such as provided by Theodore P. Dukeshire infuriates me. I was, at one time, doing a bibliography of James Hadley Chase, until I discovered about thirty titles about which I could find no information. Then Dukeshire comes up with a new title—and doesn't give the dade or pagination . . . aaaggh! (I have heard no complaints, by the way, about the fact that two-thirds of Chase's output has never been published in the United States.)

From Amy E. Goldman, 491 Mandana Blvd., #7, Oakland, CA 94610: Enclosed is a check for the back issues. Everything arrived, much quicker than I had expected (or indeed thought possible). It took me a while to get around to this letter, because I wanted to read the back issues and get up-to-date. Unfortunately, I haven't even had time to finish the current issue, so I just went back through the other issues and picked. ¶ The Saga is great! I picked up my first Stout mystery about five summers ago, and from that moment was hooked. Before the season ended, I had read every Stout book I could find—about thirty or so—and was ready for more. However, when the fall arrived I had to set my mind to more serious matters, and completely neglected finishing the rest. Since last summer I have re-read about a dozen or so, and your Saga has convinced me to read the ones I never read. Now the problem is trying to find them! ¶ In regard to your personal comments that are slipped into the Saga (I notice you've eliminated most of them), go ahead and include them. If people don't approve, they can ignore them (the comments) like I did. ¶ Which brings me to the subject of the "cruel below-the-belt disparagements concerning 20% of your subscribers." Those comments can also be ignored—as long as they don't constitute such a large proportion of the magazine that they become nauseating. I for one feel that Ms. Glantz overreacted! These days, when a male chauvinist opens his mouth to make a comment, he usually ends up with his foot in it, and I feel that if he likes chewing on his toes, let him. ¶ Surely, with around 20% of the people reading this mag being female, someone must have an interest in the female sleuth, or the women authors of mysteries. In looking at the index of reviews in volume one, I found these matters were sadly lacking. There was not a single Allingham, Bell, Aird, Christie, Cross, Disney, Mitchell, or Sayers review (not to mention others), and few for Millar, Moyes, and Lathen. Doesn't anybody out there read these authors? Or maybe it's that the ones who do are too busy reading to write. A number of good books in the genre (and some bad ones) have been written by or about women, and I hope that at least a few of them can be represented in TMF. ¶ In case you haven't remembered yet (or been told by others), the Hon Con is the Honorable Constance Ethel Morrison-Burke, written about by Joyce Porter in *A Meddlar and Her Murder*. She is a middle-aged, amateur detective, somewhat bumbling, extremely funny, and does somehow manage to correctly solve the case.

From Michael Doran, 4117 West 90th Place, Hometown, Illinois 60456: Apologies for the lengthy lapse between letters, but I got a million mitigating circumstances. The back issues arrived in good shape, and they came in handy on the very next night, when all the snow in the world fell on Chicago. Nothing like 6 hours on semi-motionless buses to broaden your reading; between these TMFs and *Variety* (which came out that day) my erudition doubled. [. . .] ¶ Anyway, those early TMFs did pique my curiosity about Harry Stephen Keeler, and your printing of my address got me some sales lists, which enabled me to satisfy that curiosity. I was only able to get one book, *The Matilda Hunter Murder*, which arrived in the mail today in all its 741-page glory. I'm pretty much of a commuter-reader (the CTA's skill at making a 20-minute trip take almost an hour is unrivalled), so this one is going to require planning and time. Still, it's nice to have things to look forward to. ¶ I'd like to say a few words about your May issue. I'd like to, but I haven't received it yet. I don't know who's to blame. If you, you should have sent some notification that the new issue would be late in coming; if the U.S. Postal Screwups, which is more likely, I may never get it. If my luck runs to form, it will be dropped into my mailbox at the exact second I drop this into the slot downtown. [*Since I haven't heard from you since my postcard, I presume that is precisely what happened.*] So I can't win. Any suggestions? [*Prayer, maybe?*] Apart from that last carp, I have no complaints about your little book, and I hope the latest postal outrage doesn't put you out of business. I'm sure we all stand ready to send along any increase that might be necessary to keep TMF coming. Hang in there.

From Bob Adey, 7 Highcroft Ave., Wordsley, Stourbridge, West Midlands, DY8 5LX, England: I've just finished reading TMF vol. 2 #2 and enjoyed it as usual. ¶ In case no one else comes up with the information, let me inform David Doerrer that "the Hon Con" is the Honourable Constance Morrison-Burke who features in at least two of Joyce Porter's books-- *Rather a Common Sort of Crime* and *A Meddler and Her Murder*. ¶ Following the Roy Winsor write-up I dug out my copy of *The Corpse that Vanished* ("Christie fans will love this one" the blurb promised) and read it. What a dreadful book! Like Walter Albert and Charles Shibuk I could find no merit in it whatsoever. Poor characterisation, unnatural dialogue, quite unbelievable characters, and the most agonising plotting I've come across. And the saddest thing is that I believe that Mr Winsor's heart is in the right place and he is trying to create a genuine whodunit series in an age that's largely forgotten them. Maybe his next book will show an improvement. ¶ A little activity to report over here on TV and radio programmes. The BBC are broadcasting new editions of 13 of the Holmes stories (starting with "The Red Headed League"). Holmes is played by Barry Foster, who also played Van der Valk for Independent Television. Also a delightfully urbane 7 part serialisation of some of the Colin Watson Flaxborough Chronicles--*Hopjoy Was Here*, *Lonelyheart 4112*, *The Flaxborough Crab* and *Coffin, Scarcely Used*. Anton Rodgers plays Purbright excellently and Brenda Bruce Miss Teatime. Best British production for ages. Se it if you get the chance.

From Larry L. French, 14326 Milbriar Circle, Chesterfield, MO 63017: Congratulations again on another outstanding issue of TMF (2/3)! ¶ I obviously enjoyed reading Marv Lachman's article on Dr. Gideon Fell (a piece of which he earlier promised and came through!) and could easily consume two or more pages responding. Suffice to say that included in my upcoming book on Carr, I have an article which talks about the unrecorded cases of Dr. Gideon Fell and much of the information in Marv's article is covered therein. I don't necessarily agree with the theory that Fell's wife was an alcoholic, but my own theory will be explained in the book. Concerning the mystery of "dates" in regard to *Death Turns the Tables*, Fell handled four cases in 1937, i.e. *To Wake the Dead* in January, *The Man Who Couldn't Shudder* in March, *Crooked Hinge* in July and *Problem of the Green Capsule* in October. Although 1936 is indicated in *Tables*, the best date I can come up with is April and May of 1938 just prior to *Till Death Do Us Part* in June of '38. 1938 was finished off in August with *Wire Cage*, when the Fells moved to Hampstead. ¶ As always, I enjoyed also the letters, reviews and the N.W.S. (and the cover was most clever).

From Bill Crider, 4206 Ninth, Brownwood, Texas 76801:
It's one of those days. After nearly a week with little to read, I've received, all at once, TMF, *Runner's World*, *The New Yorker*, *Esquire*, the new Dick Francis novel (*Risk*), and a book to review for *Best Sellers*. So why am I writing this letter: Because, by golly, Stephen Mertz and I agree on something. That might not be news to everyone, but it's news to me. Anyway, like him, I read the reviews and letters first; and the more of both, the better I like the issue. As much as I like Jeff Banks' articles, I hope you won't listen to him about letters. ¶ Not that I agree with Stephen Mertz about everything these days, but I really enjoyed his article on Carroll John Daly. I think it only fair, though probably immodest, to insist that Mr. Mertz read *my* article on Daly in *Dimensions of Detective Fiction* (Popular Press, 1976). I don't think that Daly was a very good writer as far as style, characterization, and dialogue go, but it's my contention that *The Snarl of the Beast* is the very archetype of the private-eye novel. ¶ As for the book reviewers in TMF, here again (I can't believe this) I agree with Mertz. At least about Steve Lewis. He really does good work. On the other hand, I have to admit that I also enjoy George Kelley's articles and reviews--maybe I just need an occasional dose of snide comment, but I like George's work. ¶ And thanks for the plug for *Paperback Quarterly*. Issue #2 should be a little longer that #1, and it could be longer still if we could just get some more contributors. Surely there must be someone out there who's just been dying to write on a topic related to paperbacks. If so, Billy Lee would love to print your article.

From Joe R. Lansdale, Rt. 8 Box 231, Nacogdoches, Texas 75961:
The Big Sleep finally made it to Nacogdoches and I thought the film was great, better than the original with Bogart. (Bogey fans, please do not send mail bombs. I'm also a fan of his.) There were a few minor changes, but they were very minor. One of the most faithful adaptations of a book that I've seen in ages. Locating the film in England was a strange move, but odder yet--and maybe this was the reason--it looks a lot like 1940 Los Angeles and the English cars look 40ish as well. It never bothered or distracted me because it was in England. In my mind it was always Los Angeles. The clothes in the film even seemed in step. As for the English in the film, there were few, and they could sneer and deliver their lines in excellent Chandler like manner, especially the Scotland Yard cops. ¶ Thought Mitchum was an excellent Marlowe once I got used to the idea of his age. (I had rather mixed feelings about his performance in *Farewell, My Lovely*.) He captures the side of Marlowe that is cynical, introspective and lonely. He did seem to walk through some of the wisecracks that would have been so effective if delivered by Bogart or Garner. Nonetheless, second best private eye film I've ever seen. The best being *Chinatown*. ¶ Hope a whole string of Chandler books-into-movies follow. ¶ Enjoyed your last issue very much. My favorite was the article by Steve

Mertz and second was the letter section that Jeff Banks seems to dislike. The cover was nice, crazy, but nice. Would like to see more reviews by the infamous scribner of the classic *Beak!* review. [*Don't encourage that monster!*] ¶ Glad Myrtis Broset read and liked *Fat Chance*. It's a gem of a book, very Chandler like. It surprises me how few seem to have read it, or even heard of it for that matter. Would like to let Myrtis know that there will be another Joe Shaw mystery forthcoming from Keith. It's entitled *Cop Trouble*. ¶ I'm beginning to rattle so I'll quit with one minor toot of my ego horn and a pat on the back. My first fictional sale, "The Full Count", will appear in the July issue of *Mike Shayne Mystery Magazine*. A private detective novelette, by golly. [*Congratulations! Another pro in TMF's ranks.*]

From Stephen Mertz, 153 County Road #252, Durango, CO 81301:
The May issue arrived yesterday and has already been totally devoured. That was an interesting cover, Guy. Imagine! Consumer prices rising a full 9% in only three months! What's this world coming to? ¶ A minor point at best, but I would like to make note of a typo in the reproduction of my Daly piece. The sentence in para. four should read that *Red Harvest*, *The Maltese Falcon* and *The Glass Key* are unarguably masterworks, not arguably, as appeared. [*Ouch! Mea culpa, as usual.*] The article was not meant to be an attack on Hammett but, as the title stated, a defense of Daly. ¶ I will be looking forward to Bob Adey's piece on old British paperbacks. I'd also like to encourage him to do articles on Peter Cheyney and Hank Janson. It would be interesting to see these two writers from a British perspective.

From Joe L. Hensley, 2315 Blackmore, Madison, Indiana 47250:
One thing: Someone mentioned *Writing Genre Fiction* by Dean Koontz. The name of the book is *Writing Popular Fiction*. I doubt that anyone would be confused, but perhaps. It's a useful book and every time I get someone who wants to know the easy way I suggest the book to them (along with some others) for reading and re-reading. It does make it easier because if a writer knows what he's supposed to be doing then writing can move on without too much soul searching on *whys*, *hows*, and the like. ¶ My first five from Doubleday are due to begin appearing from Condor (a new paperback house) beginning in July, then every other month thereafter.

From MRS. Gerie Frazier, 4122-A Maple Leaf Dr., New Orleans, LA 70114:
This letter is written with humor, please read it that way! ¶ The remarks from Judith Fiene and Guy's editorial comment were hilarious, and I really ought to thank you both. Believe this is the first time that I've laughed *aloud* at anything written in TMF. You are in error Judith on three counts: I am not "old", I am not a male, and I am not a "fuddy-duddy" (that spelling is from Webster's New Collegiate Dictionary). Welcome to the ranks of TMF subscribers Judity, I sincerely hope you will get as much pleasure and enjoyment from it as I do. ¶ . . . I did not respond to the first barrage of comments following the appearance of my letter in vol. 1, #6, but feel impelled to now, very briefly. Want to clarify those comments I made in the hope of pacifying the first group, and forestalling being misunderstood by future new subscribers, of which I hope there will be dozens. ¶ My comments on the reading habits of SOME women were written with humor and I truly regret that it did not come across that way to most readers. My thoughts were based on personal experience, not mere conjecture. For more than 20 years my husband's profession has taken us to many cities in many states, and to Canada, moving about once yearly. Of the count-

less women I've met, non ONE ever mentioned reading or being interested in mysteries, nor were books of this genre visible in their bookshelves. I find that somewhat incredible, and think this just might shoot down the old "law of averages"! ¶ I neither explain nor apologize for my comment on writings by Women Libbers (or persons who read them)--"to each her/his own". The remark about women reading porno was based on an article written by Dr. Joyce Brothers. "The Defense rests." ¶ Since my TMF arrived late, being forwarded from New Jersey, and you asked for letters quickly Guy, I can't make many comments on this issue other than to say that a quick once-over indicates it is another great one and I'm anxious to read it all. Most of the letters were very interesting. I particularly enjoyed the one from Ellen Nehr, whose humor is delightful--as good as Erma Bombeck. ¶ I will continue to subscribe even if you find it necessary to increase the cost. You are putting out a high quality "zine", of interest to that special breed, the "mystery buff", and I would rather spend money on TMF to satisfy this one interest of mine, instead of for regular general magazines on the open market that may, or may not, satisfy my other interests in life. ¶ I have somehow misplaced several back issues of TMF, but vaguely remember some remarks were made about letters being considered "contributions" and qualifying for a reduction in the sub rate. Personally, I feel they should NOT. I believe you asked for opinions on that, didn't you?

From Ellen Nehr, 207 S. Cassidy Ave., Bexley, Ohio 43209:
What are you trying to do to my image? I said "cook" books, as in Betty Crocker, not "comic" books. Since it was the last letter, on the last page, and probably 3:00 a.m., and because TMF was even better than your usually outstanding effort, all is forgiven. [*Thanks.*] ¶ Several readers have asked for comments or advice about dealing with dealers and/or how to go about starting a collection. I offer these remarks. ¶ It is not enough to be able to walk in a Used Book Shop for the first time and look the proprietor in the eye and to be able to say, without blushing, "Do you have any old mystery/detective novels?" Most of them look you up and down as if to X-Ray your checkbook and certify your sanity, and they say, "We have a few. What kind are you looking for?" There is the catch! Dare you drop publishers names such as Norton, Farrar and Rinehart, early Scribners (but only those with the A) or should you stick with a general off-hand line. "Mystery League, Crime Clubs, but no anthologies unless you have some early Unicorns", is as good an answer as any. He might say, "We keep THAT kind of thing in the back of the store. Any particular author?" By this time, you have more-or-less certified your credentials as a serious browser and you can rattle off, in alphabetical order (since all dealers tend to think that way), Crane, Fuller, Paul, Scherf, Stein and Taylor." Up here, in New England, two or three of those names just might ring some sort of bell even with the most iconoclastic of dealers. Most of them, skip those preliminaries, and merely point a somewhat dusty finger in the general direction of the fartherest and darkest corner and let you alone to delve into their stock while they go back to compiling a bibliography of the geneology and maps of a now extinct Massachusetts town. When you make your way forward to his desk an hour or so later with your arms loaded with respectable but unpriced books he greets you with, "Oh, are you still here? I was just about to close up." Now comes the haggle which I thoroughly and completely despise. It is seldom a case of what it is worth but, what it is worth to you, and sometimes there goes the joy of the whole expedition. Remember, anything from the 40's on up is "used" but if published before that it

is "pre-owned". If you are lucky he is glad to get them out of the shop and you can smirk all the way home because you have finally found that last volume to complete your collection of whichever author you have been looking for. The next time you walk in he might say, "Oh, you again", or "They are still in the same place and the light switch is on the wall near the back door." Now you are making progress. The next time after that, you enter boldly and he might even say "Hello" first, but it takes more than three trips to get a smile. If the majic is working, he might mention, "I've got some new ones that came out of an attic up North, and I put them aside for you in a box on the floor." Now you've got it made. ¶ That night, your husband comes home from work and says, "Guess which state we are being transferred to next month?" Please note the change of address and ignore the tear stains. . . . P.S. Steve [Lewis] has been lending me his copies of DAPA-EM and I'd love to give it a try. Since I am a devoted fan of the HIBK school do you suppose they would have me? [*We try to be tolerant of all minorities, even HIBKers.*]

(continued from page 2) of TMF's readers use. British spellings are fine if one is British, or is in Britain, or is writing for a British audience. (I wouldn't think, for instance, of altering Bob Adey's spelling.) But Martin is an American, in America, writing for a predominantly American audience, and his affectation is childish and pompous. Another of Martin's failings with which TMF's readers are not familiar (because I have been covering up for him, correcting without comment) is his apparent belief that only the first word in a book's title is capitalized. And yet Martin has the brass-balled audacity to question James Sandoe's bibliographical skills, and, what's more, he does it in an insulting manner. I could go on, but what's the point?

  Henceforth the following policy applies: contributions embodying all manner of opinion are welcomed, provided they are neither libelous nor obscene, are literately expressed and have substance, and observe at least a minimal level of decency and courtesy.

Giant Rats of Sumatra

Know all men by these presents:

GUY TOWNSEND

being deemed a Worthy Companion and Scholar of the Holmesian Canon is hereby declared a member of this ancient and benevolent society.

In Testimony Whereof we have affixed our signatures this 19TH day of JUNE, 1978.

www.ingramcontent.com/pod-product-compliance
Lightning Source LLC
Chambersburg PA
CBHW031427040426
42444CB00006B/712